D0769879

LUDWIG FEUERBACH

LUDWIG FEUERBACH

AND THE OUTCOME OF
CLASSICAL GERMAN PHILOSOPHY

BY

FREDERICK ENGELS

INTERNATIONAL PUBLISHERS
NEW YORK

ISBN 0-7178-0120-9

This printing, 1996

Edited by

C. P. DUTT

CONTENTS

FOREWORD

IN the Preface to the *Critique of Political Economy,* published in Berlin, 1859, Karl Marx relates how the two of us in Brussels in the year 1845 set about working out in common "the opposition of our view"— the materialist conception of history which was worked out especially by Marx—"to the ideological view of German philosophy, in fact to settle accounts with our previous philosophical conscience. The resolve was carried out in the form of a criticism of post-Hegelian philosophy. The manuscript, two large octavo volumes, had long reached its place of publication in Westphalia when we received the news that altered circumstances did not allow of its being printed. We abandoned the manuscript to the gnawing criticism of the mice all the more willingly since we had achieved our main purpose—to clear our own minds." [1]

Since then more than forty years have elapsed and Marx died without either of us having had an opportunity of returning to the subject. We have expressed ourselves in various places regarding our relation to Hegel, but nowhere in a comprehensive, connected account. To Feuerbach, who in many respects forms an intermediate link between Hegelian philosophy and our conception, we never returned.

In the meantime the Marxist world outlook has found representatives far beyond the boundaries of Germany and Europe and in all the languages of the civilized world. On the other hand, classical German philosophy is experiencing a kind of rebirth abroad, especially in England and Scandinavia, and even in Germany itself people appear to be getting tired of the pauper's broth of eclecticism which is ladled out in the universities there under the name of philosophy.

In these circumstances a short, connected account of our relation to

[1] Published under the title *German Ideology,* International Publishers, New York, 1939.

7

the Hegelian philosophy, of our point of departure as well as of our separation from it, appeared to me to be required more and more. Equally, a full acknowledgment of the influence which Feuerbach, more than any other post-Hegelian philosopher, had upon us during our period of storm and stress, appeared to me to be an undischarged debt of honor. I therefore willingly seized the opportunity when the editor of *Die Neue Zeit* asked me for a critical discussion of Starcke's book on Feuerbach. My contribution was published in that paper in the fourth and fifth numbers of 1886 and appears here in revised form as a separate publication.

Before sending these lines to press I have once again ferreted out and looked over the old manuscript of 1845-46. The section dealing with Feuerbach is incomplete. The completed portion consists of an exposition of the materialist conception of history which proves only how incomplete our knowledge of economic history was at that time, It contains no criticism of Feuerbach's doctrine itself; for the present purpose, therefore, it was unusable. On the other hand, in an old notebook of Marx's I have found the eleven theses on Feuerbach, printed here as an appendix. These are notes hurriedly scribbled down for later elaboration, absolutely not intended for publication, but they are invaluable as the first document in which is deposited the brilliant germ of the new world outlook.

FREDERICK ENGELS

London, February 21, 1888.

I. FROM HEGEL TO FEUERBACH[1]

THE volume[2] before us carries us back to a period which, although in time no more than a full generation behind us, has become as foreign to the present generation in Germany as if it were already a hundred years old. Yet it was the period of Germany's preparation for the Revolution of 1848, and all that has happened since then in Germany has been merely the continuation of 1848, merely the execution of the last will and testament of the revolution.

Just as in France in the eighteenth century, so in Germany in the nineteenth, a philosophical revolution ushered in the political collapse. But how different the two appeared! The French were in open combat against all official science, against the Church and often also against the State; their writings were printed across the frontier, in England or Holland, while they themselves were often in jeopardy of imprisonment in the Bastille. On the other hand, the Germans were professors, state-appointed instructors of youth; their writings were recognized textbooks, and the culminating system of the whole development—the Hegelian system—was even raised, in some degree, to the rank of a royal Prussian philosophy of state! Was it possible that a revolution could hide behind these professors, behind their obscure, pedantic phrases, their wearisome, ponderous sentences? Were not precisely those people who were then regarded as the representatives of the revolution, the liberals, the bitterest opponents of this brain-confusing philosophy? But what neither the government nor the liberals were able to see was seen at least by one man as early as 1833, and this man was indeed none other than Heinrich Heine.[3]

---

[1] Titles have been added to the numbered sections.—*Ed.*

[2] *Ludwig Feuerbach,* by C. N. Starcke, Ph. D., Stuttgart, Ferd. Enke, 1885.

[3] Engels refers to the articles *On Germany* written by the famous German poet

Let us take an example. No philosophical proposition has earned more gratitude from narrow-minded governments and wrath from equally narrow-minded liberals than Hegel's famous statement: "All that is real is rational: and all that is rational is real." That was tangibly a sanctification of things that be, a philosophical benediction bestowed upon despotism, police-government, Star Chamber proceedings and censorship. That is how Frederick William III and his subjects understood it. But according to Hegel everything that exists is certainly not also *real,* without further qualification. For Hegel the attribute of reality belongs only to that which at the same time is necessary: "The reality proves itself to be the necessary in the course of its development." A particular governmental act—Hegel himself cites the example of "a certain tax regulation"—is therefore for him by no means real without qualification. That which is necessary, however, proves itself in the last resort to be also rational; and, applied to the Prussian state of that time, the Hegelian proposition therefore merely means: this state is rational, it corresponds to reason in so far as it is necessary; and if it nevertheless appears to us to be evil, but still, in spite of its evil character, it continues to exist, then the evil character of the government is explained and justified by the corresponding evil character of the subjects. The Prussians of that day had the government that they deserved.

Now, according to Hegel, reality is, however, in no way an attribute of any given state of affairs, social or political, in all circumstances and for all time. On the contrary. The Roman Republic was real, but so was the Roman Empire which superseded it. In 1789 the French monarchy had become so unreal, that is to say, it had been so robbed of all necessity, so non-rational, that it had to be destroyed by the Great Revolution—of which Hegel always speaks with the greatest enthusiasm. In this case the monarchy was the unreal and the revolution was

Heine in which he expounded the history of the civilization of the German people for the French public. He divided it into three parts: (1) before Luther; (2) from Luther to Kant; (3) from Kant to Hegel. These articles contain his characterization of German philosophy and the role it filled in its day.—*Ed.*

the real. And so, in the course of development, all that was previously real becomes unreal, loses its necessity, its right of existence, its rationality. And in the place of moribund reality comes a new reality capable of living—peacefully if the old has enough intelligence to go to its death without a struggle; forcibly if it resists this necessity. Thus the Hegelian proposition turns into its opposite through Hegelian dialectics itself: All that is real in the sphere of human history becomes irrational in the process of time and is therefore irrational already by its destination, is tainted beforehand with irrationality, and everything which is rational in the minds of men is destined to become real, however much it may contradict the apparent reality of existing conditions. In accordance with all the rules of the Hegelian method of thought, the proposition of the rationality of everything which is real resolves itself into the other proposition: All that exists deserves to perish.[1]

But precisely here lay the true significance and the revolutionary character of the Hegelian philosophy (to which, as the close of the whole movement since Kant, we must here confine ourselves), that it once and for all dealt the deathblow to the finality of all products of human thought and action. Truth, the cognition of which is the business of philosophy, became in the hands of Hegel no longer an aggregate of finished dogmatic statements, which once discovered had merely to be learned by heart. Truth lay now in the process of cognition itself, in the long historical development of science, which mounts from lower to ever higher levels of knowledge without ever reaching, by discovering so-called absolute truth,[2] a point at which it can proceed no further and where it would have nothing more to do than to fold its hands and admire the absolute truth to which it had attained. And what holds good for the realm of philosophic knowledge holds good also for that of every other kind of knowledge and also for practical affairs. Just as knowledge is unable to reach a perfected termination in a perfect, ideal condition of humanity, so is history unable to do so; a

[1] The words of Mephistopheles in Goethe's *Faust:* "*Alles was entsteht, ist wert, dass es zugrunde geht.*"—Ed.

[2] Engels here has in view the metaphysical conception of absolute truth as completed, exhaustive knowledge, immutable for all time.—Ed.

perfect society, a perfect "state," are things which can only exist in imagination. On the contrary, all successive historical situations are only transitory stages in the endless course of development of human society from the lower to the higher. Each stage is necessary, therefore justified for the time and conditions to which it owes its origin. But in the newer and higher conditions which gradually develop in its own bosom, each loses its validity and justification. It must give way to a higher form which will also in its turn decay and perish. Just as the bourgeoisie by large-scale industry, competition and the world market dissolves in practice all stable, time-honored institutions, so this dialectical philosophy dissolves all conceptions of final absolute truth and of a final absolute state of humanity corresponding to it. For it, nothing is final, absolute, sacred. It reveals the transitory character of everything and in everything; nothing can endure before it except the uninterrupted process of becoming and of passing away, of endless ascendancy from the lower to the higher. And dialectical philosophy itself is nothing more than the mere reflection of this process in the thinking brain. It has, of course, also a conservative side: it recognizes that definite stages of knowledge and society are justified for their time and circumstances; but only so far. The conservatism of this mode of outlook is relative; its revolutionary character is absolute— the only absolute it admits.

It is not necessary, here, to go into the question of whether this mode of outlook is thoroughly in accord with the present position of natural science which predicts a possible end for the earth, and for its habitability a fairly certain one; which therefore recognizes that for the history of humanity also there is not only an ascending but also a descending branch. At any rate we still find ourselves a considerable distance from the turning point at which the historical course of society becomes one of descent, and we cannot expect Hegelian philosophy to be concerned with a subject which natural science, in its time, had not at all placed upon the agenda as yet!

But what must, in fact, be said here is this: that in Hegel the above development is not to be found in such precision. It is a necessary conclusion from his method, but one which he himself never drew with such explicitness. And this, indeed, for the simple reason that he was compelled to make a system, and, in accordance with all the traditional requirements, a system of philosophy must conclude with some sort of absolute truth. Therefore, however much Hegel, especially in his *Logic,* emphasized that this eternal truth is nothing but the logical, *i.e.,* the historical, process itself, he nevertheless finds himself compelled to make an end to this process, just because he has to bring his system to a termination at some point or other. In the *Logic* he can make this end a beginning again, since here the point of conclusion, the absolute idea [1]—which is only absolute in so far as he has absolutely nothing to say about it—"alienates," that is, transforms, itself into nature and comes to itself again later in the mind, *i.e.,* in thought and in history. But at the end of the whole philosophy a similar return to the beginning is possible only in one way, namely, by putting as the end of all history the arrival of mankind at the cognition of this self-same absolute idea, and by explaining that this cognition of the absolute idea is reached in Hegelian philosophy. In this way, however, the whole dogmatic content of the Hegelian system is declared to be absolute truth, in contradiction to his dialectical method, which dissolves all dogmatism. Thus the revolutionary side becomes smothered beneath the overgrowth of the conservative side. And what applies to philosophical cognition applies also to historical practice. Mankind, which, in the person of Hegel, has reached the point of working out the absolute idea, must also in practice have arrived so far that it can carry out this absolute idea in reality. Hence the practical political demands of the absolute idea on contemporaries may not be stretched too far. And so we find at the conclusion of the philosophy of law that the absolute idea is to be realized in that monarchy based on estates which Frederick William III so persistently but vainly promised to his subjects, *i.e.,* in a limited, moderate, indirect rule of the possessing classes suited to the petty-bourgeois German

[1] Under this Hegelian conception, the conception of god is concealed.—*Ed.*

conditions of that time. Herewith also the necessity of the nobility is demonstrated to us in a speculative fashion.

The inner necessities of the system are therefore of themselves sufficient to explain why such a thoroughly revolutionary method of thinking produced such an extremely tame political conclusion. As a matter of fact the specific form of this conclusion springs from this, that Hegel was a German, and like his contemporary Goethe had a bit of the philistine's queue dangling behind. Each of them was an Olympian Zeus in his own sphere, yet neither of them ever quite freed himself from German philistinism.

But all this did not prevent the Hegelian system from covering an incomparably greater domain than any earlier system; nor from developing in this domain a wealth of thought which is astounding even today. The *phenomenology of mind* (which one may call a parallel of the embryology and palaeontology of the mind, a development of the individual consciousness through its different stages, couched in the form of an abbreviated recapitulation of the stages through which the consciousness of man has passed in the course of history), logic, natural philosophy, philosophy of mind, and the latter worked out in its separate, historical sub-divisions: philosophy of history, of law, of religion, history of philosophy, aesthetics, etc.—in all these different historical fields Hegel labored to discover and demonstrate the pervading thread of development. And as he was not only a creative genius but also a man of encyclopaedic erudition, he played an epoch-making role in every sphere. It is self-evident that owing to the needs of the "system" he very often had to resort to those forced constructions about which his pigmy opponents make such a terrible fuss even today. But these constructions are only the frame and scaffolding of his work. If one does not loiter here needlessly, but presses on farther into the immense building, one finds innumerable treasures which today still possess undiminished value. With all philosophers it is precisely the "system" which is perishable; and for the simple reason that it springs from an imperishable desire of the human mind—the desire to overcome all contradictions. But if all contradictions are once and for all disposed of, we shall have arrived at so-called absolute truth: world history will be at an end. And yet it has to continue, although there is nothing more left for it to do—thus, a new insoluble contradiction arises. As soon as we have once realized—and in the long run no one has helped us to realize it more than Hegel himself—that the task of philosophy thus stated means nothing but the task that a single philosopher should accomplish that which can only be accomplished by the entire human race in its progressive development—as soon as we realize that, there is an end of all philosophy in the hitherto accepted sense of the word. One leaves alone "absolute truth," which is unattainable along this path or by any single individual; instead, one pursues attainable, relative truths along the path of the positive sciences, and the summation of their results by means of dialectical thinking. At any rate, with Hegel philosophy comes to an end: on the one hand, because in his system he comprehended its whole development in the most splendid fashion; and on the other hand, because, even if unconsciously, he showed us the way out of the labyrinth of "systems" to real positive knowledge of the world.

One can imagine what a tremendous effect this Hegelian system must have produced in the philosophy-tinged atmosphere of Germany. It was a triumphal procession which lasted for decades and which by no means came to a standstill on the death of Hegel. On the contrary, from 1830 to 1840 Hegelianism reigned most exclusively, and to a greater or less extent infected even its opponents. It was precisely in this period that Hegelian views, consciously or unconsciously, most extensively permeated the most diversified sciences and saturated even popular literature and the daily press from which the average "educated consciousness" derived its mental pabulum. But this victory along the whole front was only the prelude to an internal struggle.

As we have seen, the doctrine of Hegel, taken as a whole, left plenty of room for giving shelter to the most diverse practical party views. And in the theoretical Germany of that time two things above all were practical: religion and politics. Whoever placed the chief emphasis on the Hegelian *system* could be fairly conservative in both spheres; whoever regarded the dialectical *method* as the main thing could belong to the most extreme opposition, both in politics and religion. Hegel himself, despite the fairly frequent outbursts of revolutionary wrath in his works, seemed on the whole to be more inclined to the conservative side. Indeed, his system had cost him much more "bitter work of thought" than his method. Towards the end of the 'thirties, the cleavage in the school became more and more apparent. The Left wing,[1] the so-called young Hegelians, in their fight with the pietist orthodox and feudal reactionaries, abandoned bit by bit that philosophical-aristocratic reserve in regard to the burning questions of the day which up to that time had secured state toleration and even protection for their teachings. And when, in 1840, orthodox pietism and absolutist feudal reaction ascended the throne with Frederick William IV, open partisanship became unavoidable. The fight was still carried on with philosophical weapons, but no longer for abstract philosophical aims. It turned directly on the destruction of traditional religion and of the existing state. And although in the *Deutsche Jahrbücher* the practical ends were still predominantly put forward in philosophical disguise, in the *Rheinische Zeitung*[2] of 1842 the young Hegelian school revealed itself directly as the philosophy of the aspiring radical bourgeoisie and still used the meager cloak of philosophy only to deceive the censorship.

At that time, however, politics was a very thorny field, and hence the main fight came to be directed against religion; this fight, particularly since 1840, was also indirectly political. Strauss' *Life of Jesus,* published in 1835, had provided the first impulse. The theory therein

[1] In contrast to the Right Hegelians who defended the conservative views and supported autocracy, the privileged position of the nobility and the ruling religion (Protestantism,) the young, or Left, Hegelians, headed by Bruno Bauer, endeavored to draw atheist and revolutionary conclusions from Hegel's philosophy.—*Ed.*

[2] The *Deutsche Jahrbücher* [*German Annuals*] were magazines published by the Left Hegelians, A. Ruge and T. Echtermeyer, in 1838-43. The *Rheinische Zeitung* [*Rhenish Gazette*], 1842-43, was founded by Rhenish radical bourgeois. Marx was one of the main contributors to the *Gazette*. From October 1842 to the end of the year Marx was its editor-in-chief. Under Marx's leadership the *Gazette* adopted a revolutionary-democratic policy, and was suppressed by the Prussian government at the end of March 1843.—*Ed.*

developed of the formation of the gospel myths was combated later by Bruno Bauer with the proof that a whole series of evangelical stories had been fabricated by the authors themselves. The controversy between these two was carried out in the philosophical disguise of a battle between "self-consciousness" and "substance."[1] The question whether the miracle stories of the gospels came into being through an unconscious-traditional myth-creation within the bosom of the community or whether they were fabricated by the evangelists themselves was magnified into the question whether, in world history, "substance" or "self-consciousness" was the decisive driving force. Finally came Stirner, the prophet of contemporary anarchism—Bakunin has taken a great deal from him—and capped the sovereign "self-consciousness" by his sovereign "ego."[2]

We will not go further into this side of the decomposition process of the Hegelian school. More important for us is the following: the main body of the most determined young Hegelians was, by the practical necessities of its fight against positive religion, driven back to Anglo-French materialism.[3] This brought it into conflict with its school system. While materialism conceives nature as the sole reality, nature

[1] "Strauss in his book pictured Jesus as an outstanding historical personage and not as a god. Strauss considered the gospel stories to be myths which took shape in the Christian communities; he thus adhered to the opinion that these stories arose unconsciously, as it were. Bruno Bauer, in criticizing Strauss, rebuked him for not crediting consciousness with the importance due it. In Bauer's opinion, the gospel myths in the historical process of their formation passed through the consciousness of the people who had composed them intentionally to accomplish this or that religious object." (George Plekhanov.) The "self-consciousness" which the young Hegelians brought to the fore reflected the self-consciousness of the revolutionary-minded bourgeois intelligentsia of Germany during the pre-revolutionary epoch.—Ed.

[2] Engels refers to Max Stirner's (pseudonym for Caspar Schmidt) Der Einzige und sein Eigentum [The Ego and His Own], which appeared in 1845. Marx and Engels criticized it in their German Ideology.—Ed.

[3] In the seventeenth century in Great Britain and in the eighteenth century in France, natural science and materialistic philosophy developed in connection with the development of the bourgeois method of production in these countries. (Bacon, Hobbes, Locke and others were representatives of English materialism.) In France the materialist philosophers of the eighteenth century (Diderot, Helvetius, Holbach, etc.)—representatives of the revolutionary bourgeois—conducted a relentless struggle against serfdom in institutions and ideas, making use of the lessons of the English revolution while being disciples and continuers of English materialism in philosophy.—Ed.

in the Hegelian system represents merely the "alienation" of the absolute idea, so to say, a degradation of the idea. In all circumstances thinking and its thought-product, the idea, is here the primary, nature the derived element, which only exists at all by the condescension of the idea. And in this contradiction they floundered as well or as ill as they could.

Then came Feuerbach's *Essence of Christianity*. With one blow it pulverized the contradiction, in that without circumlocutions it placed materialism on the throne again. Nature exists independently of all philosophy. It is the foundation upon which we human beings, ourselves products of nature, have grown up. Nothing exists outside nature and man, and the higher beings our religious fantasies have created are only the fantastic reflection of our own essence.

The spell was broken. The "system" was exploded and cast aside. And the contradiction, shown to exist only in our imagination, was dissolved. One must himself have experienced the liberating effect of this book to get an idea of it. Enthusiasm was general; we all became at once Feuerbachians. How enthusiastically Marx greeted the new conception and how much—in spite of all critical reservations—he was influenced by it, one may read in *The Holy Family*.[1]

Even the shortcomings of the book contributed to its immediate effect. Its literary, sometimes even highflown, style secured for it a large public and was at any rate refreshing after long years of abstract and abstruse Hegelianizing. The same is true of its extravagant deifi-

---

[1] The full title of this book of Marx and Engels is: *The Holy Family, or a Criticism of Critical Criticism. Against Bruno Bauer and Co.*

"*The Holy Family* is a humorous nickname for the Bauer brothers, philosophers, and their disciples. These gentlemen preached criticism, which stands above any reality, above parties and politics, rejecting all practical activity, and only 'critically' contemplates the surrounding world and the events which take place in it. The Messrs. Bauer judged the proletariat disdainfully as an uncritical mass. Marx and Engels decidedly attacked this absurd and harmful tendency. In the name of the real human personality—the worker, downtrodden by the ruling classes and the government—they called not for contemplation but for a struggle for a better order of society. They considered, of course, the proletariat as the power that is capable of waging such a struggle and that is interested in it." (V. I. Lenin, *Marx-Engels-Marxism*, p. 38. International Publishers, New York.)—*Ed.*

cation of love, which, coming after the intolerable sovereign rule of "pure reason," had its excuse, if not justification. But what we must not forget is that it was precisely to these two weaknesses of Feuerbach that the "true socialism" which was spreading like a plague in "educated" Germany after 1844 became linked, putting literary phrases in the place of scientific knowledge, the liberation of mankind by means of "love" in place of the emancipation of the proletariat through the economic transformation of production—in short, losing itself in the nauseous fine writing and sentimentalizing typified by Herr Karl Grün.[1]

Another thing we must not forget is this: the Hegelian school was broken up, but Hegelian philosophy was not overcome through criticism; Strauss and Bauer each took one of its sides and set in polemically against the other. Feuerbach broke through the system and simply discarded it. But a philosophy is not disposed of by the mere assertion that it is false. And so powerful a work as Hegelian philosophy—which had exercised so enormous an influence on the intellectual development of the nation—did not allow itself to be disposed of by simply being ignored. It had to be "sublated" in its own sense, that is, in the sense that while its form had to be annihilated through criticism, the new content which had been won through it had to be saved. How this was brought about we shall see below.

But in the meantime the Revolution of 1848 thrust the whole of philosophy aside as unceremoniously as Feuerbach had himself thrust aside Hegel. And in the process Feuerbach himself was also pushed into the background.

[1] For a characterization of German "true socialism," see *The Communist Manifesto*, pp. 35-38, International Publishers, New York.—*Ed.*

II. IDEALISM AND MATERIALISM

THE great basic question of all philosophy, especially of modern philosophy, is that concerning the relation of thinking and being. From the very early times when men, still completely ignorant of the structure of their own bodies, under the stimulus of dream apparitions[1] came to believe that their thinking and sensation were not activities of their bodies, but of a distinct soul which inhabits the body and leaves it at death—from this time, men have been driven to reflect about the relation between this soul and the outside world. If in death it took leave of the body and lived on, there was no occasion to invent yet another distinct death for it. Thus arose the idea of its immortality which at that stage of development appeared not at all as a consolation but as a fate against which it was no use fighting, and often enough, as among the Greeks, as a positive misfortune. Not religious desire for consolation, but the quandary arising from the common universal ignorance of what to do with this soul (once its existence had been accepted) after the death of the body—led in a general way to the tedious notion of personal immortality. In an exactly similar manner the first gods arose through the personification of natural forces. And these gods in the further development of religions assumed more and more an extra-mundane form, until finally by a process of abstraction, I might almost say of distillation, occurring naturally in the course of man's intellectual development, out of the many more or less limited and mutually limiting gods there arose in the minds of men the idea of the one exclusive god of the monotheistic religions.

[1] Among savages and lower barbarians the idea is still universal that the human forms which appear in dreams are souls which have temporarily left their bodies; the real man is therefore held responsible for acts committed by his dream apparition against the dreamer. Thus B. Imthurn found this belief current, for example, among the Indians of Guiana in 1884.

Thus the question of the relation of thinking to being, the relation of spirit to nature—the paramount question of the whole of philosophy —has, no less than all religion, its roots in the narrow-minded and ignorant notions of savagery. But this question could for the first time be put forward in its whole acuteness, could achieve its full significance, only after European society had awakened from the long hibernation of the Christian Middle Ages. The question of the position of thinking in relation to being, a question which, by the way, had played a great part also in the scholasticism of the Middle Ages, the question: which is primary, spirit or nature—that question, in relation to the Church, was sharpened into this: "Did god create the world or has the world been in existence eternally?"

The answers which the philosophers gave to this question split them into two great camps. Those who asserted the primacy of spirit to nature and, therefore, in the last instance, assumed world creation in some form or other—(and among the philosophers, Hegel, for example, this creation often becomes still more intricate and impossible than in Christianity)—comprised the camp of idealism. The others, who regarded nature as primary, belong to the various schools of materialism.

These two expressions, idealism and materialism, primarily signify nothing more than this; and here also they are not used in any other sense. What confusion arises when some other meaning is put into them will be seen below.

But the question of the relation of thinking and being has yet another side: in what relation do our thoughts about the world surrounding us stand to this world itself? Is our thinking capable of the cognition of the real world? Are we able in our ideas and notions of the real world to produce a correct reflection of reality? In philosophical language this question is called the question of the "identity of thinking and being," and the overwhelming majority of philosophers give an affirmative answer to this question. With Hegel, for example, its affirmation is self-evident; for what we perceive in the real world is precisely its thought content—that which makes the world a gradual realization of the absolute idea, which absolute idea has existed somewhere from eternity, independent of the world and before the world. But it is manifest without more ado that thought can know a content which is from the outset a thought-content. It is equally manifest that what is here to be proved is already tacitly contained in the presupposition. But that in no way prevents Hegel from drawing the further conclusion from his proof of the identity of thinking and being that his philosophy, because it is correct for his own thinking, is therefore the only correct one, and that the identity of thinking and being must prove its validity by mankind immediately translating his philosophy from theory into practice and transforming the whole world according to Hegelian principles. This is an illusion which he shares with well-nigh all philosophers.

In addition there is yet another set of different philosophers—those who question the possibility of any cognition (or at least of an exhaustive cognition) of the world. To them, among the moderns, belong Hume and Kant,[1] and they have played a very important role in philosophical development. What is decisive in the refutation of this view has already been said by Hegel—in so far as this was possible from an idealist standpoint. The materialistic additions made by Feuerbach are more ingenious than profound. The most telling refutation of this as of all other philosophical fancies is practice, *viz.*, experiment and industry. If we are able to prove the correctness of our conception of a natural process by making it ourselves, bringing it into being out of its conditions and using it for our own purposes into the

---

[1] Engels calls the philosophy of Hume agnosticism. The agnostic says: I *do not know* whether there is an objective reality which is reflected by our senses. Engels calls Kant an agnostic also, who, it is true, admits of objective reality, the "thing-in-itself," but maintains that this "thing-in-itself" is beyond our ken. Engels therefore remarks: "To this Hegel, long since, has replied: If you know all the qualities of a thing, you know the thing itself; nothing remains but the fact that the said thing exists without us; and when your senses have taught you that fact, you have grasped the last remnant of the thing-in-itself, Kant's celebrated unknowable *Ding an sich.*" (Frederick Engels, *On Historical Materialism*, p. 11, International Publishers, New York.)—*Ed.*

bargain, then there is an end of the Kantian incomprehensible "thing-in-itself." The chemical substances produced in the bodies of plants and animals remained just such "things-in-themselves" until organic chemistry began to produce them one after another, whereupon the "thing-in-itself" became a thing for us, as, for instance, alizarin, the coloring matter of the madder, which we no longer trouble to grow in the madder roots in the field, but produce much more cheaply and simply from coal tar. For three hundred years the Copernican solar system was a hypothesis with a hundred, a thousand or ten thousand chances to one in its favor, but still always a hypothesis. But when Leverrier, by means of the data provided by this system, not only deduced the necessity of the existence of an unknown planet, but also calculated the position in the heavens which this planet must necessarily occupy, and when Galle really found this planet, the Copernican system was proved. If, nevertheless, the Neo-Kantians are attempting to resurrect the Kantian conception in Germany and the agnostics that of Hume in England (where in fact it had never ceased to survive), this is—in view of their theoretical and practical refutation accomplished long ago—scientifically a regression and practically merely a shamefaced way of surreptitiously accepting materialism, while denying it before the world.[1]

But during this long period from Descartes to Hegel and from Hobbes to Feuerbach, the philosophers were by no means impelled, as they thought they were, solely by the force of pure reason. On the

[1] "The principal feature of the philosophy of Kant is an attempted reconciliation of materialism and idealism, a compromise between the claims of both, a fusion of heterogeneous and contrary philosophic tendencies into one system. When Kant admits that something outside of us—a thing-in-itself—corresponds to our perceptions he seems to be a materialist. When he, however, declares this thing-in-itself to be unknowable, transcendent, 'trans-intelligible'—he appears to be an idealist. Regarding experience as the only source of our knowledge, Kant seems to be turning towards sensationalism and by way of sensationalism, under certain special conditions, toward materialism. Recognizing the apriority of space, time, and causality, etc., Kant seems to be turning towards idealism. Consistent materialists, and consistent idealists, as well as the 'pure' agnostics and Humists, criticize him for this inconsistency." (*V. I. Lenin,* "Materialism and Empirio-Criticism," *Collected Works,* Vol. XIII, p. 163, International Publishers, New York.) This dual philosophy was resurrected by the Neo-Kantians (Cohen, Natorp, etc.).—*Ed.*

contrary, what really pushed them forward was the powerful and ever more rapidly onrushing progress of natural science and industry. Among the materialists this was plain on the surface, but the idealist systems also filled themselves more and more with a materialist content and attempted pantheistically [1] to reconcile the antithesis between mind and matter. Thus, ultimately, the Hegelian system represents merely a materialism idealistically turned upside down in method and content.

It is, therefore, comprehensible that Starcke in his characterization of Feuerbach first of all investigates the latter's position in regard to this fundamental question of the relation of thinking and being. After a short introduction, in which the views of the preceding philosophers, particularly since Kant, are described in unnecessarily ponderous philosophical language, and in which Hegel, by an all too formalistic adherence to certain passages of his work, gets far less than his due, there follows a detailed description of the course of development of Feuerbach's "metaphysics" itself, as this course was reconstructed out of the sequence of those writings of this philosopher which have a bearing here. This description is industriously and carefully elaborated, only, like the whole book, it is loaded with a ballast of philosophical phraseology by no means everywhere unavoidable, which is the more disturbing in its effect the less the author keeps to the manner of expression of one and the same school, or even of Feuerbach himself, and the more he interjects expressions of very different schools— especially of the tendencies now rampant and calling themselves philosophical.

The course of evolution of Feuerbach is that of a Hegelian—a never quite orthodox Hegelian, it is true—into a materialist; an evolution which at a definite stage necessitates a complete rupture with the idealist system of his predecessor. With irresistible force Feuerbach is finally forced to the realization that the Hegelian pre-mundane existence of the "absolute idea," the "pre-existence of the logical cate-

---

[1] Pantheism—world outlook which identifies god with nature. Spinoza was one of the most prominent representatives of pantheism.—*Ed.*

gories" [1] before the world existed, is nothing more than the fantastic survival of the belief in the existence of an extra-mundane creator; that the material, sensuously perceptible world to which we ourselves belong is the only reality; and that our consciousness and thinking, however supra-sensuous they may seem, are the product of a material, bodily organ, the brain. Matter is not a product of mind, but mind itself is merely the highest product of matter. This is, of course, pure materialism. But, having got so far, Feuerbach stops short. He cannot overcome the customary philosophical prejudice, prejudice not against the thing but against the name materialism. He says: "To me materialism is the foundation of the edifice of human essence and knowledge, but to me it is not what it is to the physiologist, to the natural scientist in the narrower sense, for example, Moleschott, and necessarily so indeed from their standpoint and profession, the building itself. Backwards I fully agree with the materialists; but not forwards."

Here Feuerbach lumps together the materialism that is a general world outlook resting upon a definite conception of the relation between matter and mind, and the special form in which this world outlook was expressed at a definite stage of historical development, *viz.,* in the eighteenth century. More than that, he confuses it with the shallow and vulgarized form in which the materialism of the eighteenth century continues to exist today in the minds of naturalists and physicians, the form which was preached on their tours in the 'fifties by Büchner, Vogt and Moleschott. But just as idealism under-

---

[1] In his *Logic,* Hegel classifies the principal conceptions as follows: being, becoming, quality, quantity, essence, appearance, possibility, accident, necessity, reality, etc. These abstract basic conceptions are called "logical categories." According to Hegel, these categories have self-sustaining "eternal" existence, independent of man. In reality, conceptions and inferences are merely the reflection in man's mind of the processes going on in the material world. "Categories of Logic are factors of the cognition (ideas) of nature by man." "The practices of man, repeated a billion times, become fixed in man's consciousness as figures of logic. These figures have the endurance of prejudice, and are axiomatic in character precisely (and only) by virtue of this myriad repetition." (V. I. Lenin, *Miscellany,* Vol. IX, pp. 230 and 267, Russian edition.) The "logical categories" are precisely the ideal of which Marx speaks in the postscript to the second German edition of the first volume of *Capital:* "The ideal is nothing else than the material world reflected by the human mind and translated into forms of thought."—*Ed.*

went a series of stages of development, so also did materialism. With each epoch-making discovery even in the sphere of natural science it has to change its form; and after history also was subjected to materialistic treatment, here also a new avenue of development has opened.[1]

The materialism of the last century was predominantly mechanical, because at that time, of all natural sciences, mechanics and indeed only the mechanics of solid bodies—celestial and terrestrial—in short, the mechanics of gravity, had come to any definite close. Chemistry at that time existed only in its infantile, phlogistic form.[2] Biology still lay in swaddling clothes; vegetable and animal organisms had been only roughly examined and were explained as the result of purely mechanical causes. As the animal was to Descartes, so was man a machine to the materialists of the eighteenth century. This exclusive application of the standards of mechanics to processes of a chemical and organic nature—in which processes, it is true, the laws of me-

[1] In this connection it is important to remember the following words of Joseph Stalin:

"Engels said that 'materialism must take on a new aspect with each new great discovery.' We all know that none other than Lenin fulfilled this task, as far as his own time was concerned, in his remarkable work, *Materialism and Empirio-Criticism*.

"It is well known that Plekhanov, who loved to chaff Lenin for his 'lack of concern' for matters of philosophy, did not even dare to make a serious attempt to undertake such a task."

It is this "new aspect" of materialism given by Lenin to the dialectical materialism of Marx and Engels which is properly designated as the "Leninist stage of Marxian philosophy." The "new aspect" of materialism developed by Lenin is, of course, nothing more than the further development of the philosophy of Marx and Engels according to the development of the sciences, primarily of the natural sciences, in the epoch in which Lenin lived. This must be accentuated, inasmuch as the Social-Democrats distort the facts by maintaining that Marxist philosophy and its Leninist aspect differ from one another.—*Ed.*

[2] According to this theory, the essence of combustion consisted in this: that a burning body gives off a special igneous substance called phlogiston. At the end of the eighteenth century, scientists were groping for another explanation of the process of combustion. Lavoisier, a French chemist, taking advantage of certain suggestions made by Priestley, an English chemist, advanced the theory that during combustion no secret substance such as phlogiston was being given off by the burning body, but that, on the contrary, a separate element, oxygen, unites with the burning body. By this discovery, as Engels says, Lavoisier "placed chemistry, which... had so long stood on its head, on its feet for the first time." (Frederick Engels, "From the Preface to *Capital*, Volume II," Karl Marx, *Selected Works*, Vol. I, p. 348, International Publishers, New York.)—*Ed.*

chanics are also valid, but are pushed into the background by other and higher laws—constitutes a specific but at that time inevitable limitation of classical French materialism.

The second specific limitation of this materialism lay in its inability to comprehend the universe as a process—as matter developing in an historical process. This was in accordance with the level of the natural science of that time, and with the metaphysical, *i.e.,* anti-dialectical manner of philosophizing connected with it. Nature, it was known, was in constant motion. But according to the ideas of that time, this motion turned eternally in a circle and therefore never moved from the spot; it produced the same results over and over again. This conception was at that time inevitable. The Kantian theory of the origin of the solar system [1] had been put forward but recently and was regarded merely as a curiosity. The history of the development of the earth, geology, was still totally unknown, and the conception that the animate natural beings of today are the result of a long sequence of development from the simple to the complex could not at that time scientifically be put forward at all. The unhistorical view of nature was therefore inevitable. We have the less reason to reproach the philosophers of the eighteenth century on this account, since the same thing is found in Hegel. According to him, nature, as a mere "alienation" of the idea, is incapable of development in time—capable only of extending its manifoldness in space, so that it displays simultaneously and alongside of one another all the stages of development comprised in it, and is condemned to an eternal repetition of the same process. This absurdity of a development in space, but outside of time—the fundamental condition of all development—Hegel imposes upon nature just at the very time when geology, embryology, the physiology of plants and animals, and organic chemistry were being built up, and when everywhere on the basis of these new sciences brilliant foreshadowings of the later theory of evolution were appearing (*e.g.,* Goethe and Lamarck). But the system demanded it; hence the

---

[1] The theory which holds that the sun and the planets originated from revolving, incandescent nebulous masses.—*Ed.*

method, for the sake of the system, had to become untrue to itself.

This same unhistorical conception prevailed also in the domain of history. Here the struggle against the remnants of the Middle Ages blurred the view. The Middle Ages were regarded as a mere interruption of history by a thousand years of universal barbarism. The great progress made in the Middle Ages—the extension of the area of European culture, the bringing into existence there of great nations, capable of survival, and, finally, the enormous technical progress of the fourteenth and fifteen centuries—all this was not seen. Consequently a rational insight into the great historical inter-connections was made impossible and history served at best as a collection of examples and illustrations for the use of philosophers.

The vulgarizing peddlers who in Germany in the 'fifties busied themselves with materialism by no means overcame the limitations of their teachers. All the advances of natural science which had been made in the meantime served them only as new proofs against the existence of a creator of the world; and, in truth, it was quite outside their scope to develop the theory any further. Though idealism was at the end of its tether and was dealt a death blow by the Revolution of 1848, it had the satisfaction of seeing that materialism had for the moment fallen lower still. Feuerbach was unquestionably right when he refused to take responsibility for this materialism; only he should not have confounded the doctrines of these hedge-preachers with materialism in general.[1]

Here, however, two things must be pointed out.

First, during Feuerbach's lifetime, natural science was still involved in a process of violent fermentation—which only during the last fifteen years has reached a relatively clear conclusion. New scientific data were acquired to a hitherto unheard-of extent, but the establishing of inter-relations, and thereby the bringing of order into this chaos of discoveries following closely upon each other's heels has only quite recently become possible for the first time. It is true that Feuerbach had lived to

---

[1] See pages 65-69 of this volume for the portion of manuscript omitted by Engels in the original publication of *Ludwig Feuerbach.—Ed.*

see all three of the decisive discoveries—that of the cell, the transformation of energy and the theory of evolution named after Darwin. But how could the lonely philosopher, living in rural solitude, be able sufficiently to follow scientific developments in order to appreciate at their full value discoveries which scientists themselves at that time either contested or did not adequately know how to make use of? The blame for this falls solely upon the wretched conditions in Germany, in consequence of which cobweb-spinning eclectic flea-crackers had taken possession of the chairs of philosophy, while Feuerbach, who towered above them all, had to rusticate and grow sour in a little village. It is therefore not Feuerbach's fault that the historical conception of nature, which had now become possible and which removed all the one-sidedness of French materialism, remained inaccessible to him.

Secondly, Feuerbach is quite correct in asserting that the exclusively natural-scientific materialism was indeed "the foundation of the edifice of human ... knowledge, but ... not ... the building itself." For we live not only in nature but also in human society, and this also no less than nature has its history of development and its science. It was therefore a question of bringing the science of society (*i.e.*, the sum total of the so-called historical and philosophical sciences) into harmony with the materialist foundation, and of reconstructing it thereupon. But it did not fall to Feuerbach's lot to do this. In spite of the "foundation," he remained here bound by the traditional idealist fetters, a fact which he recognizes in these words: "Backwards I ... agree with the materialists; but not forwards!" But it was Feuerbach himself who did not go "forward" here, in the social domain, who did not get beyond his standpoint of 1840 or 1844. And this indeed was again chiefly due to this isolation—which compelled him, who, of all philosophers, was the most inclined to social intercourse, to produce thoughts out of his solitary head instead of in amicable and hostile encounters with other men of his own caliber. Later we shall see in detail how much he remained an idealist in this sphere.

It need only be added here that Starcke looks for Feuerbach's idealism in the wrong place. "Feuerbach is an idealist; he believes in the progress of mankind" (p. 19). "The foundation, the substructure of the whole, remains nevertheless idealism. Realism for us is nothing more than a protection against wrong paths, while we follow our ideal trends. Are not compassion, love and enthusiasm for truth and justice ideal forces?" (p. *viii.*)

In the first place, idealism here means nothing but the pursuit of "ideal" aims. But these necessarily have to do at the most with Kantian idealism and its "categorical imperative,"[1] but Kant himself called his philosophy "transcendental idealism" by no means because he dealt therein also with moral ideals, but for quite other reasons, as Starcke will remember. The superstition that philosophical idealism is pivoted round a belief in moral, *i.e.,* social, "ideals," arose outside philosophy, among the German philistines who learned by heart from Schiller's poems the few morsels of philosophical culture they needed. No one has criticized more severely the impotent "categorical imperative" of Kant—impotent because it demands the impossible, and therefore never attains to any reality—no one has more cruelly derided the philistine sentimental enthusiasm for unrealizable ideals purveyed by Schiller than the complete idealist Hegel. (See, for example, his *Phenomenology.*)

In the second place, we cannot get away from the fact that everything that sets men acting must find its way through their brain—even eating and drinking, which begins as a consequence of the sensation of hunger or thirst transmitted through the brain, and ends as a result of the sensation of satisfaction likewise transmitted through the brain. The influences of the external world upon man express themselves in his brain, are reflected therein as feelings, thoughts, instincts, volitions—in short, as "ideal tendencies," and in this form become "ideal powers." If, then, a man is converted into an idealist because he

---

[1] In Kantian philosophy this is the term applied to the unconditional obligation which forms the so-called highest moral law of pure reason, *a priori*, in its very nature. According to the idealistic doctrine of Kant, this law is immutable, established for all eternity and imperatively prescribes human conduct. The Kantian practical philosophy was basically only the abstract ideological expression of bourgeois morality with all the marks of the weakness and immaturity of the German bourgeoisie.—*Ed.*

"follows ideal tendencies" and admits that "ideal powers" have an influence over him—then every person who is at all normally developed is a born idealist and how, in that case, can there still be any materialists?

In the third place, the conviction that humanity, at least at the present moment, moves on the whole in a progressive direction has absolutely nothing to do with the antithesis between materialism and idealism. The French materialists equally with the deists [1] Voltaire and Rousseau held this conviction to an almost fanatical degree, and often made the greatest personal sacrifices for it. If ever anybody dedicated his whole life to the "enthusiasm for truth and justice"—using this phrase in the good sense—it was Diderot. If, therefore, Starcke declares all this to be "idealism," this merely proves that the word materialism has lost all meaning for him—as has also the whole antithesis between the two standpoints.

The fact is that Starcke, although perhaps unconsciously, in this makes an unpardonable concession to the traditional philistine prejudice against the word materialism resulting from the long-continued defamation by the priests. By the word materialism the philistine understands gluttony, drunkenness, lust of the eye, lust of the flesh, arrogance, cupidity, avarice, miserliness, profit-hunting and stock-exchange swindling—in short, all the filthy vices in which he himself indulges in private. By the word idealism he understands the belief in virtue, universal philanthrophy and in a general way a "better world" of which he boasts before others, but in which he himself at the utmost believes only so long as he is going through the depression or bankruptcy consequent upon his customary "materialist" excesses. It is then

---

[1] Deism—a philosophical school inimical to the positive religions with their cult of a personal god but which does not completely reject the idea of god. This school retains god as the original cause of everything, as the force which gives the first impulse. The deists do not break finally with the idea of god as do the consistent materialists (who are atheists). The deists recognize a god who plays the same role as the king under the English constitution who is limited by laws which he cannot revoke without Parliament. Similarly the god of the deists, who according to them created nature, is limited by the laws of nature and cannot act arbitrarily, create miracles in contravention of these laws. Thus deism afforded the possibility of recognizing the conclusions of materialism in inconsistent, concealed form.—*Ed.*

that he sings his favorite song, "What is man?—Half beast! Half angel!"

For the rest, Starcke takes great pains to defend Feuerbach against the attacks and doctrines of the vociferous lecturers who today go by the name of philosophers in Germany. For people who are interested in this afterbirth of German classical philosophy this is a matter of importance; for Starcke himself it may have appeared necessary. We, however, will spare the reader this.

III. FEUERBACH'S PHILOSOPHY
OF RELIGION AND ETHICS

THE real idealism of Feuerbach becomes evident as soon as we come to his philosophy of religion and ethics. He by no means wishes to abolish religion: he wants to perfect it. Philosophy itself must be absorbed in religion. "The periods of humanity are distinguished only by religious changes. A historical movement is fundamental only when it is rooted in the hearts of men. The heart is not a form of religion, so that the latter should exist also in the heart; the heart is the essence of religion." (Quoted by Starcke, p. 168, German edition.) According to Feuerbach, religion is the relation based on the affections, the relation based on the heart, between man and man, which until now has sought its truth in a fantastic reflection of reality—in the fantastic reflection of human qualities through the medium of one or many gods. But now it finds its truth directly and without any intermediary in the love between the "I" and the "Thou." Thus, finally, with Feuerbach sex love becomes one of the highest forms, if not the highest form, of the practice of his religion.

Now relations between man and man, based on affection, and especially between the sexes, have existed as long as mankind has. Sex love in particular has undergone a development and won a place during the last eight hundred years which has made it a compulsory pivotal point of all poetry during this period. The existing positive religions have limited themselves in this matter to the bestowal of a higher consecration upon state-regulated sex love (*i.e.,* upon the marriage laws) and they could all disappear completely tomorrow without changing in the slightest the practice of love and friendship. The Christian religion in France was, as a matter of fact, so completely swept away in the years 1793-98 that even Napoleon could not re-introduce it without opposition and difficulty; and this without any desire for a substitute, in Feuerbach's sense, making itself felt in the interval.

Feuerbach's idealism consists here in this: he does not simply accept mutual relations based on reciprocal inclination between human beings, such as sex love, friendship, compassion, self-sacrifice, etc., as what they are in themselves—without associating them with any particular religion which to him, too, belongs to the past; but instead he asserts that they will come to their full realization for the first time as soon as they are consecrated by the name of religion. The chief thing for him is not that these purely human relations exist, but that they shall be conceived of as the new, true religion. They are to have full value only after they have been marked with a religious stamp. Religion is derived from *religare* and meant originally "a bond." Therefore, every bond between two men is a religion. Such etymological tricks are the last resource of idealist philosophy. Not what the word has meant according to the historical development of its actual use, but what it ought to mean according to its derivation is what counts. And so sex love and the intercourse between the sexes is apotheosized to a "religion," merely in order that the word religion, which is so dear to idealistic memories, may not disappear from the language. The Parisian reformers of the type of Louis Blanc [1] used to speak in precisely the same way in the 'forties. They likewise could conceive of a man without religion only as a monster, and used to say: *"Donc, l'athéisme c'est votre réligion!"* [2] If Feuerbach wishes to establish a true religion upon the basis of an essentially materialist conception of nature, that is the same as regarding modern chemistry as true alchemy. If religion can exist without its god, alchemy can exist without its philosopher's stone. By the way, there exists a very close connection between alchemy and religion. The philosopher's stone has many god-like properties and

[1] The so-called Social-Democrats dealt with in Section IV of *The Communist Manifesto*, p. 43.—*Ed.*

[2] Well, then, atheism is your religion!—*Ed.*

the Egyptian-Greek alchemists of the first two centuries of our era contributed their share to the development of Christian doctrines, as the data given by Kopp and Berthelot have proved.

Feuerbach's assertion that "the periods of human development are distinguished only by religious changes" is decidedly false. Great historical turning points have been *accompanied* by religious changes only so far as the three world religions which have existed up to the present —Buddhism, Christianity and Islam—are concerned. The old primitive tribal and national religions did not proselytize and lost all their power of resistance as soon as the independence of the tribe or people was lost. For the Germans it was sufficient to have simple contact with the decaying Roman Empire and with its newly adopted Christian world religion which fitted its economic, political and ideological conditions. Only with these more or less artificially created world religions, particularly Christianity and Islam, do we find that general historical movements acquire a religious imprint. Even in regard to Christianity the religious stamp in revolutions of really universal significance is restricted to the first stages of the struggle for the emancipation of the bourgeoisie—from the thirteenth to the seventeenth centuries—and is to be accounted for not as Feuerbach thinks by the hearts of men and their religious needs but by the entire previous history of the Middle Ages which knew no other form of ideology than religion and theology. But when the bourgeoisie of the eighteenth century was strengthened enough likewise to possess an ideology of its own, suited to its own class standpoint, it made its great and conclusive revolution, the French, appealing exclusively to juristic and political ideas, and troubling itself with religion only in so far as this stood in its way. But it never occurred to it to put a new religion in place of the old. Everyone knows how Robespierre failed in his attempt.

The possibility of purely human sentiments in the intercourse with other human beings has nowadays been sufficiently curtailed by the society in which we live, which is based upon class antagonism and class rule. We have therefore no reason to curtail it still more by exalting these sentiments to a religion. And similarly the understanding of the great historical class struggles has already been sufficiently obscured by current historiography, particularly in Germany, so that there is also no need for us to make such an understanding totally impossible by transforming the history of these struggles into a mere appendix of ecclesiastical history. Already here it becomes evident how far today we have moved beyond Feuerbach. His "finest passages" in glorification of his new religion of love are totally unreadable to-day.

The only religion which Feuerbach examines seriously is Christianity, the world religion of the Occident based upon monotheism. He proves that the Christian god is only a fantastic reflection, a mirror-image, of man. Now, this god is, however, himself the product of a tedious process of abstraction, the concentrated quintessence of the numerous earlier tribal and national gods. And man, whose image this god is, is therefore also not a real man, but likewise the quintessence of the numerous real men, man in the abstract, therefore himself again a mental image. The same Feuerbach who, on every page, preaches sensuousness, absorption in the concrete, in actuality, becomes thoroughly abstract as soon as he begins to talk of any other than mere sex relations between human beings.

Of these relations only one aspect appeals to him: morality. And here Feuerbach's astonishing poverty when compared with Hegel again becomes striking. The latter's ethics or doctrine of moral conduct is the philosophy of law and embraces: (1) abstract right; (2) morality; (3) moral conduct under which again are comprised: the family, civil society and the state. Here the content is as realistic as the form is idealistic. Besides morality the whole sphere of law, economy, politics is here included. With Feuerbach it is just the reverse. In form he is realistic since he takes his start from man; but there is absolutely no mention of the world in which this man lives; hence this "man" remains always the same abstract man who occupied the field in the philosophy of religion. For this man is not born of woman: he issues, as from a chrysalis, from the god of the monotheistic religions. He therefore does not live in a real world historically created and historically determined. It is true he has intercourse with other men, but each one of them is, however, just as much an abstraction as he himself is. In the *Philosophy of Religion* we still had men and women, but in the *Ethics* even this last distinction disappears altogether. Feuerbach, to be sure, at long intervals makes such statements as: "A man thinks differently in a palace and in a hut." "If because of hunger, of misery, you have no foodstuff in your body, you likewise have no stuff for morality in your head or heart." "Politics must become our religion," etc. But Feuerbach is absolutely incapable of achieving anything with these remarks. They remain purely figures of speech; and even Starcke has to admit that for Feuerbach politics constituted an impassable frontier and the "science of society, sociology, was *terra incognita* to him."

He appears just as superficial, in comparison with Hegel, in his treatment of the antithesis of good and evil. "One believes one is saying something great," Hegel remarks, "if one says that 'man is naturally good.' But one forgets that one says something far greater when one says 'man is naturally evil.'" According to Hegel, evil is the form in which the motive force of historical development presents itself. This, indeed, contains the twofold significance that while, on the one hand, each new advance necessarily appears as a sacrilege against things hallowed, as a rebellion against conditions which, however old and moribund, have still been sanctified by custom; on the other hand, it is precisely the wicked passions of man—greed and lust for power—which, since the emergence of class antagonisms, serve as levers of historical development—a fact of which the history of feudalism and of the bourgeoisie, for example, constitutes a single continual proof. But it does not occur to Feuerbach to investigate the historical role of moral evil. To him history is altogether a mysterious domain in which he feels ill at ease. Even his dictum: "Man as he sprang originally from nature was only a mere creature of nature, not a man. Man is a product of men, of culture, of history"—even this dictum with him remains absolutely sterile.

What Feuerbach has to tell us about morals can, therefore, only be extremely meager. The urge towards happiness is innate in man, and must therefore form the basis of all morals. But the urge towards happiness is subject to a double correction. First, by the natural consequences of our actions: after the debauch come the "blues," and habitual excess is followed by illness. Secondly, by its social consequences: if we do not respect the similar urge of other people towards happiness they will defend themselves, and so interfere with our own urge towards happiness.

Consequently, in order to satisfy our urge, we must be in a position to appreciate rightly the results of our conduct and must likewise allow others an equal right to seek happiness. Rational self-restraint with regard to ourselves, and love—again and again love!—in our intercourse with others—these are the basic laws of Feuerbach's morality; from them all others are derived. And neither the most talented utterances of Feuerbach nor the strongest eulogies of Starcke can hide the tenuity and superficiality of these few propositions.

Only very exceptionally, and in no case to his and other people's profit, can an individual satisfy his urge towards happiness by preoccupation with himself. Rather it requires preoccupation with the outside world, means to satisfy his needs, that is to say, means of subsistence, an individual of the opposite sex, books, conversation, argument, activities, objects for use and working up. Feuerbach's morality either presupposes that these means and objects of satisfaction are given to every individual as a matter of course, or else it offers only inapplicable good advice and is therefore not worth a brass farthing to people who are without these means. And Feuerbach himself states this in the dry words: "A man thinks differently in a palace and in a hut. If because of hunger, of misery, you have no foodstuff in your body you likewise have no stuff for morality in your head or heart."

Do matters fare any better in regard to the equal right of others to the pursuit of happiness? Feuerbach posed this claim as absolute, as holding good in all times and circumstances. But since when has it been valid? Was there ever in antiquity between slaves and masters, or in the Middle Ages between serfs and barons, any talk about an equal right to the pursuit of happiness? Was not the urge towards happiness of the oppressed class sacrificed ruthlessly and "by right of law" to the interests of the ruling class?—Yes, that was indeed immoral; nowadays, however, equality of rights is recognized—recognized in words, since the bourgeoisie, in its fight against feudalism and in the development of capitalist production, was compelled to abolish all privileges of estate, *i.e.,* personal privileges, and to introduce the equality of all individuals before the law, first in the sphere of private law, then gradually also in the sphere of state law. But the urge towards happiness thrives only to a trivial extent on ideal rights. To the greatest extent of all it thrives on material means; and capitalist production takes care to ensure that the great majority of those with equal rights shall get only what is essential for bare existence. Capitalist production has therefore little more respect, if indeed any more, for the "equal right to the pursuit of happiness" of the majority than had slavery or serfdom. And are we better off in regard to the mental means to happiness, the educational means? Is not "the schoolmaster of Sadowa" [1] himself a mythical person?

More than that. According to Feuerbach's theory of morals the Stock Exchange is the highest temple of moral conduct provided only that one always speculates correctly! If my urge towards happiness leads me to the Stock Exchange, and if there I correctly gauge the consequences of my actions so that only agreeable results and no disadvantages ensue, that is, if I always win, then I am fulfilling Feuerbach's precept. Moreover, I do not thereby interfere with the equal right of another person to pursue his happiness: for that other man went to the Exchange just as voluntarily as I did and in concluding the speculative transaction with me he has followed his urge towards happinness as I have followed mine. Should he lose his money, then by that very fact his activity is proved to have been immoral, because of his bad reckoning, and since I have given him the punishment he deserves, I can even slap my chest proudly, like a modern Rhada-

---

[1] The victory of Königgrätz (Sadowa) was called a victory of the Prussian schoolmaster, *i.e.,* of the superior Prussian culture.—*Ed.*

manthus.[1] Love, too, rules on the Stock Exchange, in so far as it is not simply a sentimental figure of speech, for each finds in others the satisfaction of his own urge towards happiness, which is just what love ought to achieve and how it acts in practice. And if I gamble with correct prevision of the consequences of my operations, and therefore with success, I fulfill all the strictest injunctions of Feuerbachian morality— and become a rich man into the bargain. In other words, Feuerbach's morality is cut exactly to the pattern of modern capitalist society, little as Feuerbach himself might imagine or desire it.

But love!—yes, with Feuerbach, love is everywhere and at all times the wonder-working god who should help to surmount all difficulties of practical life—and at that in a society which is split into classes with diametrically opposite interests. At this point the last relic of its revolutionary character disappears from the philosophy, leaving only the old cant: Love one another—fall into each other's arms regardless of distinctions of sex or estate—a universal orgy of reconciliation.

In short, the Feuerbachian theory of morals fares like all its predecessors. It is designed to suit all periods, all peoples and all conditions, and precisely for that reason it is never and nowhere applicable. It remains, as regards the real world, as powerless as Kant's categorical imperative. In reality every class, even every profession, has its own morality, and even this it violates whenever it can do so with impunity. And "love," which is to unite all, manifests itself in wars, altercations, lawsuits, domestic broils, divorces and every possible exploitation of one by another.

Now how was it possible that the powerful impetus given by Feuerbach turned out to be so unfruitful for himself? For the simple reason that Feuerbach himself never contrives to escape from the realm of abstraction—for which he has a deadly hatred—into that of living reality. He clings hard to nature and humanity; but nature and humanity remain always mere words with him. He is incapable of telling us anything definite either about real nature or real men.

---

[1] According to Greek mythology, Rhadamanthus was appointed judge in hell because of his righteousness.—*Ed.*

But from the abstract men of Feuerbach one arrives at real living men only when one considers them as participants in history. And that is what Feuerbach resisted, and therefore the year 1848, which he did not understand, signified for him merely the final break with the real world, retirement into solitude. The blame for this again chiefly falls on the conditions then obtaining in Germany, which condemned him to rot away miserably.

But the step which Feuerbach did not take nevertheless had to be taken. The cult of abstract man which formed the kernel of Feuerbach's new religion had to be replaced by the science of real men and of their historical development. This further development of Feuerbach's standpoint beyond Feuerbach himself was inaugurated by Marx in 1845 in *The Holy Family*.

IV. DIALECTICAL MATERIALISM

STRAUSS, Bauer, Stirner, Feuerbach—these were the offshoots of Hegelian philosophy, in so far as they did not abandon the field of philosophy. Strauss, after his *Life of Jesus* and *Dogmatics,* produced only literary studies in philosophy and ecclesiastical history after the fashion of Renan. Bauer only achieved something in the field of the history of the origin of Christianity, though what he did here was important. Stirner remained a curiosity, even after Bakunin blended him with Proudhon and labeled the blend "anarchism." Feuerbach alone was of significance as a philosopher. But not only did philosophy— claimed to soar above all sciences and to be the all comprehensive science of sciences—remain for him an impassable barrier, an unassailable holy thing, but as a philosopher, too, he stopped halfway; the lower half of him was materialist, the upper half idealist. He was incapable of disposing of Hegel through criticism; he simply threw him aside as useless, while he himself, compared with the encyclopaedic wealth of the Hegelian system, achieved nothing positive beyond a grandiloquent religion of love and a meager, impotent system of morals.

Out of the dissolution of the Hegelian school, however, there developed still another tendency, the only one which has borne real fruit. And this tendency is essentially connected with the name of Marx.[1]

[1] Here I may be permitted to make a personal explanation. Lately repeated reference has been made to my share in this theory, and so I can hardly avoid saying a few words here to settle this particular point. I cannot deny that both before and during my forty years' collaboration with Marx I had a certain independent share in laying the foundations, and more particularly in elaborating the theory. But the greater part of its leading basic principles, particularly in the realm of economics and history, and, above all, its final, clear formulation, belong to Marx. What I contributed—at any rate with the exception of a few special studies—Marx could very well have done without me. What

The separation from the Hegelian school was here also the result of a return to the materialist standpoint. That means it was resolved to comprehend the real world—nature and history—just as it presents itself to everyone who approaches it free from pre-conceived idealist fancies. It was decided relentlessly to sacrifice every idealist fancy which could not be brought into harmony with the facts conceived in their own and not in a fantastic connection. And materialism means nothing more than this. But here the materialistic world outlook was taken really seriously for the first time and was carried through consistently—at least in its basic features—in all domains of knowledge concerned.

Hegel was not simply put aside. On the contrary, one started out from his revolutionary side described above, from the dialectical method. But in its Hegelian form this method was unusable. According to Hegel, dialectics is the self-development of the concept. The absolute concept does not only exist—where unknown—from eternity, it is also the actual living soul of the whole existing world. It develops into itself through all the preliminary stages which are treated at length in the *Logic* and which are all included in it. Then it "alienates" itself by changing into nature, where, without consciousness of itself, disguised as the necessity of nature, it goes through a new development and finally comes again to self-consciousness in man. This self-consciousness then elaborates itself again in history from the crude form until finally the absolute concept again comes to itself completely in the Hegelian philosophy. According to Hegel, therefore, the dialectical development apparent in nature and history, *i.e.,* the casual interconnection of the progressive movement from the lower to the higher, which asserts itself through all zig-zag movements and temporary setbacks, is only a miserable copy of the self-movement of the concept going on from eternity, no one knows where, but at all events in-

Marx accomplished I would not have achieved. Marx stood higher, saw further, and took a wider and quicker view than all the rest of us. Marx was a genius; we others were at best talented. Without him the theory would not be what it is today. It therefore rightly bears his name.

dependently of any thinking human brain. This ideological reversal had to be done away with. We comprehended the concepts in our heads once more materialistically—as images of real things instead of regarding the real things as images of this or that stage of development of the absolute concept. Thus dialectics reduced itself to the science of the general laws of motion—both of the external world and of human thought—two sets of laws which are identical in substance, but differ in their expression in so far as the human mind can apply them consciously, while in nature and also up to now for the most part in human history, these laws assert themselves unconsciously in the form of external necessity in the midst of an endless series of seeming accidents. Thereby the dialectic of the concept itself became merely the conscious reflex of the dialectical motion of the real world and the dialectic of Hegel was placed upon its head; or rather, turned off its head, on which it was standing before, and placed upon its feet again. And this materialist dialectic which for years has been our best working tool and our sharpest weapon was, remarkably enough, discovered not only by us, but also independently of us and even of Hegel by a German worker, Joseph Dietzgen.[1]

In this way, however, the revolutionary side of Hegelian philosophy was again taken up and at the same time freed from the idealist trammels which in Hegel's hands had prevented its consistent execution. The great basic thought that the world is not to be comprehended as a complex of ready-made *things,* but as a complex of *processes,* in which the things apparently stable no less than their mind-images in our heads, the concepts, go through an uninterrupted change of coming into being and passing away, in which, in spite of all seeming accidents and of all temporary retrogression, a progressive development asserts itself in the end—this great fundamental thought has, especially since the time of Hegel, so thoroughly permeated ordinary consciousness that in this generality it is scarcely ever contradicted. But to

[1] See *Das Wesen des menschlichen Kopfarbeit, dargestellt von einem Handarbeiter* [*The Nature of Human Brainwork, Described by an Artisan*]. Another critique of pure and practical reason. Hamburg, Meissner, 1869.

acknowledge this fundamental thought in words and to apply it in reality in detail to each domain of investigation are two different things. If, however, investigation always proceeds from this standpoint, the demand for final solutions and eternal truths ceases once for all; one is always conscious of the necessary limitation of all acquired knowledge, of the fact that it is conditioned by the circumstances in which it was acquired. On the other hand, one no longer permits oneself to be imposed upon by the antitheses, insuperable for the still common old metaphysics, between true and false, good and bad, identical and different, necessary and accidental. One knows that these antitheses have only a relative validity; that that which is recognized now as true has also its latent false side which will later manifest itself, just as that which is now regarded as false has also its true side by virtue of which it could previously have been regarded as true. One knows that what is maintained to be necessary is composed of sheer accidents and that the so-called accidental is the form behind which necessity hides itself—and so on.

The old method of investigation and thought which Hegel calls "metaphysical," which preferred to investigate *things* as given, as fixed and stable, a method the relics of which still strongly haunt people's minds, had a good deal of historical justification in its day. It was necessary first to examine things before it was possible to examine processes. One had first to know what a particular thing was before one could observe the changes going on in connection with it. And such was the case with natural science. The old metaphysics which accepted things as finished objects arose from a natural science which investigated dead and living things as finished objects. But when this investigation had progressed so far that it became possible to take the decisive step forward of transition to the systematic investigation of the changes which these things undergo in nature itself, then the last hour of the old metaphysics sounded in the realm of philosophy also. And in fact, while natural science up to the end of the last century was predominantly a *collecting* science, a science of finished things, in our century it is essentially a *classifying science,* a science of the processes, of the origin and development of these things and of the interconnection which binds all these natural processes into one great whole. Physiology, which investigates the processes occurring in plant and animal organisms; embryology, which deals with the development of individual organisms from germ to maturity; geology, which investigates the gradual formation of the earth's surface—all these are the offspring of our century.

But, above all, there are three great discoveries which have enabled our knowledge of the interconnection of natural processes to advance by leaps and bounds: first, the discovery of the cell as the unit from whose multiplication and differentiation the whole plant and animal body develops—so that not only is the development and growth of all higher organism recognized to proceed according to a single general law, but also, in the capacity of the cell to change, the way is pointed out by which organisms can change their species and thus go through a more than individual development. Second, the transformation of energy, which has demonstrated that all the so-called forces operative in the first instance in inorganic nature—mechanical force and its complement, so-called potential energy, heat, radiation (light or radiant heat), electricity, magnetism and chemical energy—are different forms of manifestation of universal motion, which pass into one another in definite proportions so that in place of a certain quantity of the one which disappears, a certain quantity of another makes its appearance and thus the whole motion of nature is reduced to this incessant process of transformation from one form into another. Finally, the proof which Darwin first developed in connected form that the stock of organic products of nature surrounding us today, including mankind, is the result of a long process of evolution from a few original unicellular germs, and that these again have arisen from protoplasm or albumen which came into existence by chemical means.

Thanks to these three great discoveries and the other immense advances in natural science, we have now arrived at the point where we can demonstrate as a whole the interconnection between the processes in nature not only in particular spheres but also in the interconnection of these particular spheres themselves, and so can present in an approximately systematic form a comprehensive view of the interconnection in nature by means of the facts provided by empirical natural science itself. To furnish this comprehensive view was formerly the task of so-called natural philosophy. It could do this only by putting in place of the real but as as yet unknown interconnections ideal and imaginary ones, filling out the missing facts by figments of the mind and bridging the actual gaps merely in imagination. In the course of this procedure it conceived many brilliant ideas and foreshadowed many later discoveries, but it also produced a considerable amount of nonsense, which indeed could not have been otherwise. Today, when one needs to comprehend the results of natural scientific investigation only dialectically, that is, in the sense of their own interconnections, in order to arrive at a "system of nature" sufficient for our time; when the dialectical character of this interconnection is forcing itself against their will even into the metaphysically-trained minds of the natural scientists, today this natural philosophy is finally disposed of. Every attempt at resurrecting it would be not only superfluous but a *step backwards.*

But what is true of nature, which is hereby recognized also as a historical process of development, is also true of the history of society in all its branches and of the totality of all sciences which occupy themselves with things human (and divine). Here, too, the philosophy of history, of law, of religion, etc., has consisted in the substitution of an interconnection fabricated in the mind of the philosopher for the actual interconnection to be demonstrated in the events; and in the comprehension of history as a whole as well as in its separate parts, as the gradual realization of ideas—and, indeed, naturally always the pet ideas of the philosopher himself. According to this, history worked unconsciously but with necessity towards a certain predetermined, ideal goal—as, for example, according to Hegel, towards the realization of his absolute idea—and the unalterable trend towards this absolute idea formed the inner interconnection in the events of history. A new mysterious providence—unconscious or gradually coming into consciousness—was thus put in the place of the real, still unknown inter-connection. Here, therefore, just as in the realm of nature, it was necessary to do away with these fabricated, artificial interconnections by the discovery of the real ones; a task which ultimately amounts to the discovery of the general laws of motion which assert themselves as the ruling ones in the history of human society.

In one point, however, the history of the development of society proves to be essentially different from that of nature. In nature—in so far as we ignore man's reactions upon nature—there are only blind unconscious agencies acting upon one another and out of whose interplay the general law comes into operation. Nothing of all that happens—whether in the innumerable apparent accidents observable upon the surface of things, or in the ultimate results which confirm the regularity underlying these accidents—is attained as a consciously desired aim. In the history of society, on the other hand, the actors are all endowed with consciousness, are men acting with deliberation or passion, working towards definite goals; nothing happens without a conscious purpose, without an intended aim. But this distinction, important as it is for historical investigation, particularly of single epochs and events, cannot alter the fact that the course of history is governed by inner general laws. For here, also, on the whole, in spite of the consciously desired aims of all individuals, accident apparently reigns on the surface. That which is willed happens but rarely; in the majority of instances the numerous desired ends cross and conflict with one another, or these ends themselves are from the outset in-capable of realization or the means of attaining them are insufficient. Thus the conflict of innumerable individual wills and individual actions in the domain of history produces a state of affairs entirely analogous to that in the realm of unconscious nature. The ends of the actions are intended, but the results which actually follow from these actions are not intended; or when they do seem to correspond to the end intended, they ultimately have consequences quite other than those intended. Historical events thus appear on the whole to be like-wise governed by chance. But where on the surface accident holds sway, there actually it is always governed by inner, hidden laws and it is only a matter of discovering these laws.

Men make their own history, whatever its outcome may be, in that each person follows his own consciously desired end, and it is precisely the resultant of these many wills operating in different directions and of their manifold effects upon the outer world that constitutes history. Thus it is also a question of what the many individuals desire. The will is determined by passion or deliberation. But the levers which immediately determine passion or deliberatioin are of very different kinds. Partly they may be external objects, partly ideal motives, ambition, "enthusiasm for truth and justice," personal hatred or even purely individual whims of all kinds. But, on the one hand, we have seen that the many individual wills active in history for the most part produce results quite other than those they intended—often quite the opposite; their motives therefore in relation to the total result are likewise of only secondary significance. On the other hand, the further question arises: What driving forces in turn stand behind these motives? What are the historical causes which transform themselves into these motives in the brains of the actors?

The old materialism never put this question to itself. Its conception of history, in so far as it has one at all, is therefore essentially pragmatic; it judges everything according to the motives of the action; it divides men in their historical activity into noble and ignoble and then finds that as a rule the noble are defrauded and the ignoble are victorious. Hence it follows for the old materialism that nothing very edifying is to be got from the study of history, and for us, that in the realm of history the old materialism becomes untrue to itself because it takes the ideal driving forces which operate there as ultimate causes, instead of investigating what is behind them, what are the driving forces of these driving forces. The inconsistency does not lie in the fact that *ideal* driving forces are recognized, but in the investigation not being carried further back behind these into their motive causes. On the other hand, the philosophy of history, particularly as represented by Hegel, recognizes that the ostensible and also the really operating motives of men who figure in history are by no means the ultimate causes of historical events; that behind these motives are other motive forces, which have to be discovered. But it does not seek these forces in history itself, it imports them rather from outside, from out of philosophical ideology, into history. Hegel, for example, instead of explaining the history of ancient Greece out of its own inner interconnections, simply maintains that it is nothing more than the working out of "types of beautiful individuality," the realization of a "work of art" as such. He says much in this connection about the old Greeks that is fine and profound but that does not prevent us today from refusing to be put off with such an explanation, which is a mere manner of speech.

When, therefore, it is a question of investigating the driving forces which—consciously or unconsciously, and indeed very often unconsciously—lie behind the motives of men in their historical actions and which constitute the real ultimate driving forces of history, then it is not a question so much of the motives of single individuals, however eminent, as of those motives which set in motion great masses, whole peoples, and again whole classes of the people in each people; and here, too, not the transient flaring up of a straw-fire which quickly dies down, but a lasting action resulting in a great historical transformation. To ascertain the driving causes which here in the minds of acting masses and their leaders—the so-called great men—are reflected as conscious motives, clearly or unclearly, directly or in ideological, even glorified form—that is the only path which can put us on the track of the laws holding sway both in history as a whole, and at particular periods and in particular lands. Everything which sets men in motion must go through their minds; but what form it will take in the mind will depend very much upon the circumstances. The workers have by no means become reconciled to capitalist machine industry, even though they no longer simply break the machines to pieces as they still did in 1848 on the Rhine.

But while in all earlier periods the investigation of these driving causes of history was almost impossible—on account of the complicated and concealed interconnections between them and their effects—our present period has so far simplified these interconnections that the riddle could be solved. Since the establishment of large-scale industry, *i.e.,* at least since the peace of Europe in 1815, it has been no longer a secret to any man in England that the whole political struggle there has turned on the claims to supremacy of two classes: the landed aristocracy and the middle class. In France, with the return of the Bourbons, the same fact was perceived; the historians of the Restoration period, from Thierry to Guizot, Mignet and Thiers, speak of it everywhere as the key to the understanding of all French history since the Middle Ages. And since 1830 the working class, the proletariat, has been recognized in both countries as a third competitor for power. Conditions had become so simplified that one would have had to close one's eyes deliberately not to see in the fight of these three great classes and in the conflict of their interests the driving force of modern history—at least in the two most advanced countries.

But how did these classes come into existence? If it was possible at first glance still to ascribe the origin of the great, formerly feudal landed property—at least in the first instance—to political causes, to taking possession by force, this could no longer be done in regard to the bourgeoisie and the proletariat. Here the origin and development of two great classes was seen to lie clearly and palpably in purely economic causes. And it was just as clear that in the struggle between landed property and the bourgeoisie, no less than in the struggle between the bourgeoisie and the proletariat, it was a question in the first instance of economic interests, to the furtherance of which political power was intended to serve merely as a means. Bourgeoisie and proletariat both arose in consequence of a transformation of the economic conditions, more precisely, of the mode of production. The transition, first from guild handicrafts to manufacture, and then from manufacture to large-scale industry, with steam and mechanical power, had caused the development of these two classes. At a particular stage the new forces of production set in motion by the bourgeoisie—in the first place the division of labor and the combination of many workers, each producing a particular part, in one complete manufacture—and the conditions and requirements of exchange, developed through these productive forces, became incompatible with the existing order of production historically established and sanctified by law, that is to say, incompatible with the privileges of the guild and the numerous other local and personal privileges (which were only so many fetters to the unprivileged) of the feudal social organization. The forces of production represented by the bourgeoisie rebelled against the order of production represented by the feudal landlords and the guild-masters. The result is known: the feudal fetters were smashed, gradually in England, at one blow in France. In Germany the process is not yet finished. But just as, at a definite stage of its development, manufacture came into conflict with the feudal order of production, so now big industry has already come into conflict with the bourgeois order of production established in its place. Tied down by this order, by the narrow limits of the capitalist mode of production, big industry produces on the one hand an ever increasing proletarianization of the great mass of the people, and on the other hand an ever greater mass of unsalable products. Overproduction and mass misery, each the cause of the other—that is the absurd contradiction which is its outcome, and which of necessity calls for the liberation of the productive forces by means of a change in the mode of production.

In modern history at least it is therefore proved that all political struggles are class struggles, and all class struggles for emancipation in the last resort, despite their necessarily political form—for every class struggle is a political struggle—turn ultimately on the question of economic emancipation. Therefore, here at least, the state—the political order—is the subordinate, and civil society—the realm of economic relations—the decisive element. The traditional conception, to which Hegel, too, pays homage, saw in the state the determining element, and in civil society the element determined by it. Appearances correspond to this. As all the driving forces of the actions of any individual person must pass through his brain, and transform themselves into motives of his will in order to set him into action, so also all the needs of civil society—no matter which class happens to be the ruling one—must pass through the will of the state in order to secure general validity in the form of laws. That is the formal aspect of the matter—the one which is self-evident. The question arises, however, what is the content of this merely formal *will*—of the individual as well as of the state—and whence is this content derived? Why is just this intended and not something else? If we inquire into this we discover that in modern history the will of the state is, on the whole, determined by the changing needs of civil society, by the supremacy of this or that class, in the last resort, by the development of the productive forces and relations of exchange.

But if already in our modern era, with its gigantic means of production and communication, the state is not an independent domain with an independent development, but one whose stock as well as development is to be explained in the last resort by the economic conditions of life of the society, then this must be still more true of earlier times when the production of the material life of man was not carried on with these abundant auxiliary means, and when, therefore, the necessity of such production must necessarily have exercised a still greater mastery over men. If the state today, in the era of big industry and of railways, is on the whole only a reflex, in comprehensive form, of the economic needs of the class controlling production, then this must have been much more so in an epoch when each generation of men was forced to spend a far greater part of its aggregate lifetime in satisfying material needs, and was therefore much more dependent on them than we are today. An examination of the history of earlier periods, as soon as it is seriously undertaken from this angle, most abundantly confirms this. But, of course, this cannot be gone into here.

If the state and public law are determined by economic relations, so, too, of course is private law [1] which indeed in essence sanctions

[1] The division always made by bourgeois law itself. Public law deals with state institutions, the structure of the administrative apparatus and the political rights of citizens. Civil or private law is mainly concerned with the property rights of citizens (law of property, of debts, of family, of inheritance).—*Ed.*

only the existing economic relations between individuals which are normal in the given circumstances. The form in which this happens can, however, vary considerably. It is possible, as happened in England, in harmony with the whole national development, to retain in the main the forms of the old feudal laws while giving them a bourgeois content; in fact, directly giving a bourgeois meaning to the old feudal name. But, also, as happened in Western continental Europe, Roman Law, the first world law of a commodity-producing society, with its unsurpassably acute elaboration of all the essential legal relations of simple commodity owners (of buyers and sellers, debtors and creditors, contracts, obligations, etc.) can be taken as a foundation. In this case, for the benefit of a still petty-bourgeois and semi-feudal society, it can be adapted to the situation of such a society either simply through every-day legal practice (the common law) or, with the help of allegedly enlightened, moralizing jurists a special law code can be worked out out from it to correspond with such social conditions— a code which in these circumstances will also be a bad one from a legal standpoint *(e.g.,* the Prussian *Landrecht).* Whereby again after the great bourgeois revolution, such a classic law code of bourgeois society as the French *Code Civil* [1] can be worked out upon the basis of this same Roman Law. If, therefore, bourgeois legal regulations merely express the economic life-conditions of society in legal form, then this can take place well or ill according to circumstances.

The state presents itself to us as the first ideological power over mankind. Society creates for itself an organ for the safeguarding of its general interests against internal and external attacks. This organ is the state power. Hardly come into being, this organ makes itself independent in regard to society; and, indeed, the more so, the more it becomes the organ of a particular class, the more it directly enforces the supremacy of that class. The fight of the oppressed class against the ruling class becomes necessarily a political fight, a fight first of all against the political dominance of this class. The consciousness of the

[1] The bourgeois law code issued under Napoleon I which became a model for legislation in other countries.—*Ed.*

interconnection between this political struggle and its economic roots becomes dulled and can be lost altogether. While this is not altogether the case with the participants, it almost always happens with the historians. Of the ancient sources on the struggles within the Roman Republic only Appian [1] tells us clearly and distinctly what was at issue in the last resort—namely, landed property.

But once the state has become an independent power in regard to society, it produces forthwith a further ideology. It is indeed only among professional politicians, theorists of constitutional law and jurists of private law, that the connection with economic facts gets completely lost. Since in each particular case the economic facts must assume the form of juristic motives in order to receive legal sanction; and since, in so doing, consideration of course has to be paid to the whole legal system already in operation, the consequence is that the juristic form is made everything and the economic content nothing. Public law and private law are treated as independent spheres, each having its own independent historical development, each being capable of and needing a systematic presentation by the thoroughgoing elimination of all inner contradictions.

Still higher ideologies, that is, such as are still further removed from the material, economic basis, take the form of philosophy and religion. Here the interconnection between the ideas and their material condition of existence becomes more and more complicated, more and more obscured by intermediate links. But the interconnection exists. Just as the whole Renaissance period from the middle of the fifteenth century was an essential product of the towns and therefore of the bourgeoisie so also was the subsequently newly awakened philosophy. Its content was in essence only the philosophical expression of the thoughts corresponding to the development of the small and middle bourgeoisie into a big bourgeoisie. Among last century's Englishmen and Frenchmen who in many cases were just as much

[1] Roman historian of the second century who wrote mainly about the civil wars of ancient Rome.—*Ed.*

political economists as philosophers, this is clearly evident; and we have proved it above in regard to the Hegelian school.

We will now in addition deal only briefly with religion, since the latter appears to stand furthest away from, and to be the most foreign to, material life. Religion arose in very primitive times from erroneous and primitive ideas of men about their own nature and that of the external world surrounding them. Every ideology, however, once it has arisen, develops in connection with the given concept-material, and develops this material further; otherwise it would cease to be ideology, that is, occupation with thoughts as with independent entities, developing independently and subject only to their own laws. That the material life conditions of the persons inside whose heads this thought process goes on, in the last resort determine the course of this process, remains of necessity unknown to these persons, for otherwise there would be an end to all ideology. These primitive religious notions, therefore, which in the main are common to each group of kindred peoples, develop, after the separation of the group, in a manner peculiar to each people, according to the living conditions falling to their lot. For a number of groups of peoples, and particularly for the Aryans (so-called Indo-Europeans) this process has been shown in detail by comparative mythology. The gods so created by each people were national gods, whose domain extended no farther than the national territory which they were to defend; on the other side of its boundaries other gods held undisputed sway. The idea of them could only continue to exist as long as the nation existed; they fell with its fall. The Roman world empire, the economic conditions of whose origin we do not need to examine here, brought about this downfall of the old nationalities. The old national gods decayed, even those of the Romans, which themselves also were fashioned only to suit the narrow confines of the city of Rome. The need to complement the world empire by means of a world religion was clearly revealed in the attempts made to provide in Rome recognition and altars for all the foreign gods to the slightest degree respectable alongside of the indigenous ones. But a new world religion is not to be made in this fashion, by imperial decree. The new world religion, Christianity, had already quietly come into being, out of a mixture of generalized Oriental, particularly Jewish, theology and vulgarized Greek, particularly Stoic, philosophy. What it originally looked like has to be first laboriously discovered again, since its official form, as it has been handed down to us, is merely that in which it became a state religion, to which purpose it was adapted by the Council of Nicaea. The fact that already after two hundred and fifty years it became a state religion suffices to show that it was a religion in correspondence with the conditions of the time. In the Middle Ages, in the same measure as feudalism developed, it grew into the religious counterpart to it, with a corresponding feudal hierarchy. And as the bourgeoisie arose, there developed within it, in opposition to feudal Catholicism, the Protestant heresy, which first appeared in Southern France, among the Albigenses[1] at the time of the highest flourishing of the cities there. The Middle Ages had attached to theology all the other forms of ideology —philosophy, politics, jurisprudence—and made them sub-divisions of theology. It thereby constrained every social and political movement to take on a theological form. To the masses whose minds were fed with religion to the exclusion of all else, it was necessary to put forward their own interests in a religious guise in order to produce a great agitation. And since the bourgeoisie from the beginning brought into being an appendage of propertyless urban plebeians, day-laborers and servants of all kinds, belonging to no recognized social estate, precursors of the later proletariat, so likewise heresy soon became divided into a bourgeois moderate heresy and a plebeian revolutionary one, the latter an abomination to the bourgeois heretics themselves.

The ineradicability of the Protestant heresy corresponded to the

[1] The Albigenses, Cathari, participated in a movement which covered Southern France during the twelfth and thirteenth centuries. (The name is derived from the town of Albi, in the south of France.) The movement was directed against the exploiting Roman Catholic church headed by the Pope. The urban trading bourgeoisie, the artisans, the city poor and the peasants all took part in the movement. In the beginning of the twelfth century a special crusade was organized by the Pope against the Albigenses resulting in protracted warfare (lasting over 20 years) and ending with the defeat of the Albigenses.—Ed.

invincibility of the rising bourgeoisie. When the bourgeoisie had become sufficiently strengthened, its struggle against the feudal nobility, which till then had been predominantly local, began to assume national dimensions. The first great action occurred in Germany—the so-called Reformation. The bourgeoisie was neither powerful enough nor sufficiently developed to be able to unite under its banner the rest of the rebellious estates—the plebeians of the towns, the lower nobility and the peasants on the land. At first the nobles were defeated; the peasants rose in a revolt which forms the peak of the whole revolutionary struggle; the cities left them in the lurch, and thus the revolution succumbed to the armies of the secular princes who reaped the whole profit.[1] Thenceforward Germany disappears for three centuries from the ranks of countries playing an independent part in history. But besides the German, Luther, appeared the Frenchman, Calvin. With true French acumen he put the bourgeois character of the reformation in the forefront, republicanized and democratized the church. While the Lutheran reformation in Germany degenerated and reduced the country to rack and ruin, the Calvinist reformation served as a banner for the republicans in Geneva, in Holland and in Scotland, freed Holland from Spain and from the German empire and provided the ideological costume for the second act of the bourgeois revolution which took place in England. Here Calvinism justified itself as the true religious disguise of the interests of the bourgeoisie of that time, and on this account did not reach full acceptance, as the revolution was completed in 1689 by a compromise between one part of the nobility and the bourgeoisie. The English state church was re-established; but not in its earlier form of a Catholicism which had the king for its pope, being, instead, strongly Calvinized. The old state church had celebrated the merry Catholic Sabbath and had fought against the dull Calvinist one. The new bourgeois church introduced the latter, which adorns England to this day.

In France, the Calvinist minority was suppressed in 1685 and either

---

[1] See Frederick Engels, *The Peasant War in Germany*, International Publishers, New York.—*Ed.*

Catholicized or driven out of the country. But what was the good? Already at that time the free-thinker Pierre Bayle was at work, and in 1694 Voltaire was born. The forcible measures of Louis XIV only made it easier for the French bourgeoisie to carry through its revolution in the irreligious and exclusively political form which alone was suited to the developed bourgeoisie. Instead of Protestants, free-thinkers took their seats in the national assemblies. Thereby Christianity entered into its final stage. It had become incapable for the future of serving any progressive class as the ideological garb of its aspirations. It became more and more the exclusive possession of the ruling classes and these apply it as a mere means of government, to keep the lower classes within limits. For this each of the different classes uses its own appropriate religion: the landowning class—Catholic Jesuitism or Protestant orthodoxy; the liberal and radical bourgeoisie—rationalism; and it makes little difference whether these gentlemen themselves believe in their respective religions or not.

We see, therefore: religion, once formed, always contains traditional material, just as in all ideological domains tradition forms a great conservative force. But the transformations which this material undergoes spring from class relations, that is to say, out of the economic relations of the persons who execute these transformations. And here that is sufficient.

In the above it could only be a question of giving a general sketch of the Marxist conception of history, at most with a few illustrations as well. The proof is to be found in history itself; and in this regard I may be permitted to say that it has been sufficiently furnished in other writings. This conception, however, puts an end to philosophy in the realm of history, just as the dialectical conception of nature made all natural philosophy both unnecessary and impossible. It is no longer a question anywhere of inventing interconnections from out of our brains, but of discovering them in the facts. For philosophy, which has been expelled from nature and history, there remains only the realm of pure thought (so far as it is left): the theory of the laws of the thought process itself, logic and dialectics.

With the Revolution of 1848, "educated" Germany said farewell to theory and went over to the field of practice. Small production, based upon handicraft and manufacture, were superseded by really large-scale industry. Germany again appeared on the world market. The new little German empire abolished at least the more crying of the anomalies which had been placed in the way of its development by the system of petty states, the relics of feudalism and bureaucratic economy. But to the same degree that speculation abandoned the philosopher's study in order to set up its temple in the Stock Exchange, educated Germany lost the great aptitude for theory which had been the glory of Germany in the days of its deepest political humiliation— the aptitude for purely scientific investigation, irrespective of whether the result obtained was practically applicable or not, whether likely to meet with the approval or disapproval of the police authorities. Official German natural science, it is true, maintained its position in the front rank, particularly in the field of specialized research. But already the American journal, *Science,* remarks with truth that the decisive advances in the sphere of the comprehensive correlation of particular facts and their generalization into laws, are now being made much more in England, instead of, as formerly, in Germany. And in the sphere of the historical sciences, philosophy included, the old fearless zeal for theory has now disappeared completely, along with classical philosophy. Empty eclecticism and an anxious concern for career and income, descending to the most vulgar place-hunting, occupies its place. The official representatives of these sciences have become the undisguised ideologists of the bourgeoisie and the existing state— but at a time when both stand in open antagonism to the working class.

Only among the working class does the German aptitude for theory remain unimpaired. Here it cannot be exterminated. Here there is no concern for careers, for profit-making, or for gracious patronage from above. On the contrary, the more ruthlessly and disinterestedly science proceeds the more it finds itself in harmony with the interests and efforts of the workers. The new tendency, which recognized that the key to the understanding of the whole history of society lies in the historical development of labor, from the outset addressed itself by preference to the working class and here found the response which it neither sought nor expected from officially recognized science. The German working class is the inheritor of German classical philosophy.

APPENDICES

Frederick Engels

An Omitted Fragment From *Ludwig Feuerbach*[1]

THE vulgarizing peddlers who busied themselves with materialism in Germany during the 'fifties by no means overcame the limitations of their teachers. All the advances of natural science which had been made in the meantime served them as new proofs against belief in a creator of the world, and, indeed, it was quite outside their scope to develop theory any further. Idealism was hard hit by 1848, but materialism in this new shape sank to even lower depths. Feuerbach was certainly right to disclaim responsibility for *this* materialism; but he should not have lumped together the doctrines of the hedge-preachers and materialism in general.

At about the same time, however, empirical natural science made such an advance and achieved such brilliant results that not only did it become possible to overcome completely the mechanical one-sidedness of the eighteenth century, but natural science itself was, through the proof of the inter-relation existing in nature itself between the various spheres of investigation (mechanics, physics, chemistry, biology, etc.), transformed from an empirical into a theoretical science and, by the integration of the results achieved, into a system of materialistic knowledge of nature. The mechanics of gases; newly created organic chemistry, which stripped the last remnants of incomprehensibility from the so-called organic compounds, one after the other, by preparing them from inorganic materials; the science of embryology which dates back to 1818; geology, palaeontology and the comparative anatomy of plants and animals—all of them provided new material to an unprecedented

[1] See footnote on p. 28.—*Ed.*

extent. Three great discoveries, however, were of decisive importance.

The first was the proof of the transformation of energy obtained from the discovery of the mechanical equivalent of heat (by Robert Mayer, Joule and Colding). All the innumerable operative causes in nature, which until then had led a mysterious inexplicable existence as so-called "forces"—mechanical force, heat, radiation (light and radiant heat), electricity, magnetism, the force of chemical combination and dissociation—are now proved to be special forms, modes of existence of one and the same energy, *i.e.*, motion. We are not only able to demonstrate their perpetual transformation in nature from one form into another, but we can carry out this transformation itself in the laboratory and in industry, and this in such a way that a given quantity of energy in one form always corresponds to a given quantity of energy in this or that other form. Thus we can express the unit of heat in kilogram-meters, and again the units of any quantity of electrical or chemical energy in units of heat and vice versa. Similarly we can measure the consumption and supply of energy to a living organism, and express these in any unit desired, *e.g.*, in units of heat. The unity of all motion in nature is no longer a philosophical assertion but a fact of natural science.

The second—chronologically earlier—discovery was that of the organic cell by Schwann and Schleiden—of the cell as the unit, out of the multiplication and differentiation of which all organisms, except the very lowest, arise and develop. With this discovery, the investigation of the organic, living products of nature—comparative anatomy and physiology, as well as embryology—was for the first time put upon a firm foundation. The mystery was removed from the origin, growth and structure of organisms. The hitherto incomprehensible miracle resolved itself into a process taking place according to a law essentially identical for all multi-cellular organisms.

But an essential gap still remained. If all multi-cellular organisms—plants as well as animals, including man—grow from a single cell according to the law of cell-division, whence, then, comes the infinite variety of these organisms? This question was answered by the third great discovery, the theory of evolution, which was first presented in connected form and substantiated by Darwin. However numerous the modifications in details this theory will yet undergo, it nevertheless, on the whole, already solves the problem in a more than satisfactory manner. The evolutionary series of organisms from few and simple to increasingly manifold and complex forms, as we see them today before our eyes, right up to and including man himself, has been proved in all its main basic features. Thereby not only has an explanation been made possible for the existing stock of the organic products of nature, but the basis has been given for the pre-history of the human mind, for following all its various stages of evolution from the protoplasm, simple and structureless yet responsive to stimuli, of the lower organisms right up to the thinking human brain. Without this pre-history, however, the existence of the thinking human brain remains a miracle.

With these three great discoveries, the main processes of nature are explained and traced back to natural causes. Only one thing remains to be done here: to explain the origin of life from inorganic nature. At the present stage of science, that means nothing else than the preparation of albuminous bodies from inorganic materials. Chemistry is approaching ever closer to this task. It is still a long way from it. But when we reflect that it was only in 1828 that the first organic body, urea, was prepared by Wöhler from inorganic materials and that innumerable so-called organic compounds are now artificially prepared without any organic substances, we shall not be inclined to bid chemistry halt before the production of albumen. Up to now, chemistry has been able to prepare any organic substance the composition of which is accurately known. As soon as the composition of albuminous bodies shall have become known, it will be possible to proceed to the production of live albumen. But that chemistry should achieve over night what nature herself even under very favorable circumstances could succeed in doing on a few planets after millions of years—would be to demand a miracle.

The materialist conception of nature, therefore, stands today on very different and firmer foundations than in the last century. Then it was only the motion of the heavenly bodies and of rigid terrestrial bodies under the influence of gravity that was thoroughly understood to some extent. Almost the whole sphere of chemistry and the whole of organic nature remained an incomprehensible secret. Today, the whole of nature is laid open before us as a system of interconnections and processes which have been, at least in their main features, explained and comprehended. Indeed, the materialistic outlook on nature means no more than simply conceiving nature just as it exists without any foreign admixture, and as such it was understood originally among the Greek philosophers as a matter of course. But between those old Greeks and us lie more than two thousand years of an essentially idealistic world outlook, and hence the return to the self-evident is more difficult than it seems at first glance. For the question is not at all one of simply repudiating the whole thought-content of those two thousand years but of criticizing it in order to extricate from within the false, but for its time and the process of evolution even inevitable, idealistic form, the results gained from this transitory form. And how difficult that is, is demonstrated for us by those numerous scientists who are inexorable materialists within their science but who, outside it, are not only idealists but even pious, nay orthodox, Christians.

All these epoch-making advances in natural science passed Feuerbach by without essentially touching him. This was not so much his fault as that of the wretched conditions in Germany by virtue of which the professorial chairs at the universities had been seized on by empty-headed, eclectic flea-crackers, while Feuerbach, who towered high above them all, was forced almost to rusticate in the lonely isolation of a village. Hence it was that on the subject of nature—along with a few brilliant aphorisms—he was so much engaged in threshing belletristic straw. Thus, he says: "Life is certainly not the product of a chemical process, nor at all of an isolated natural force or phenomenon, to which the metaphysical materialist reduces life; it is a result of the whole of nature." That life is a result of the whole of nature in no way contradicts the circumstance that while albumen, which is the sole dependent carrier of life, arises under definite conditions determined by the whole inter-connectedness of nature, it nevertheless arises as the product of a chemical process. (Had Feuerbach lived under circumstances which would have permitted him to follow the development of science even superficially, he would never have committed the blunder of speaking of a chemical process as of the effect of an isolated natural force.) It is to be ascribed to the same seclusion when Feuerbach loses himself in a series of barren speculations, turning round in a circle, on the relation of thinking to the organ of thought, the brain—a territory into which Starcke follows him with predilection.

Enough has been said. Feuerbach is opposed to the name materialism. And not entirely without justification, for he never quite sheds his idealism. In the sphere of nature he is a materialist, but in the sphere of human....

[*Here the fragment ends.*]

Frederick Engels

Karl Marx's *Contribution*
to the Critique of Political Economy[1]

IN all scientific spheres, the Germans have long since demonstrated their equality with, and in most of them their superiority over, the remaining civilized nations. Only one science was not able to count on a single German name among its adepts, *viz.,* political economy. The reason is obvious. Political economy is the theoretical analysis of modern bourgeois society and therefore presupposes developed bourgeois conditions, conditions which in Germany, after the wars of the Reformation and the peasant wars, particularly after the Thirty Years' War,[2] could not arise for centuries. The separation of Holland from the Empire forced Germany to the rear in world trade and from the outset reduced its industrial development to the scantiest proportions. While the Germans were slowly and laboriously recovering from the devastation of the civil wars, while they were using up all their bourgeois energy, which had never been very great, in fruitless struggle against the customs barriers and idiotic trade regulations which every

[1] This review by Engels of Marx's *Contribution to the Critique of Political Economy* (1859) appeared in London in 1895 in the German periodical *Das Volk.* A concluding article did not appear owing to the cessation of the journal. In the present edition the text is reproduced completely and corresponds with the original of the London periodical.—*Ed.*

[2] The Thirty Years' War was waged on German soil under religious slogans (Catholicism against Protestantism) in the first half of the seventeenth century between various changing groupings of German principalities, kingdoms and the imperial power (Catholic). Non-German armies also participated in the war, chiefly Swedish on the Protestant side and French and Spanish on the Catholic side. The war wrought terrible ravages throughout the country, intensified still further its political dismemberment and held back its economic development for a long time.—*Ed.*

petty princeling and imperial baron imposed on the industry of his
subjects, while the imperial towns with their guild ceremonials and
patrician cliques were falling into decay—Holland, England and
France conquered the leading positions in world trade, amassed colony
after colony and developed the manufacturing industry to the highest
pitch, until finally England, owing to steam power which first im-
parted value to its coal and iron deposits, attained the foremost position
in modern bourgeois development. So long, however, as a struggle
had still to be waged against such ludicrously antiquated relics of the
Middle Ages as up to 1830 laid fetters on the material bourgeois development of Germany, no German political economy was possible.
Only with the establishment of the Customs Union [1] did the Germans
arrive at a position in which they could at all even *understand* political
economy. From this time, in fact, began the importation of English
and French political economy for the benefit of the German bourgeoisie. Presently the intelligentsia and bureaucracy seized hold of the
imported material and worked it up in a fashion not very creditable
to the "German spirit." From the medley of industrial barons, traders,
schoolmasters and bureaucrats engaged in authorship there arose a
German economic literature which in its insipidity, shallowness, lack
of thought, verbosity and plagiarism was paralleled only by the German novel. Among the people with practical aims, the protectionist
school of the industrialists was the first to establish itself; and its
authority, List, is still the best that German bourgeois-economic literature has produced, although the whole of his glorious work is copied
from the Frenchman, Ferrier, the theoretical originator of the Continental System.[2] In opposition to this tendency there arose in the 'forties
the free school of the traders in the Baltic provinces, who, with childish
but self-interested faith, echoed the arguments of the English free
traders. Finally, among the schoolmasters and bureaucrats who had to

---

[1] The German *Customs and Trade Union* was established on January 1, 1834, between Prussia and the other German states with the exception of Austria.—*Ed.*

[2] The Continental System was the policy pursued by Napoleon I of prohibiting the
import of English goods on the Continent.—*Ed.*

deal with the theoretical side of the subject, there were to be found dried-up, uncritical herbarium collectors like Herr Rau, speculating wiseacres like Herr Stein, who translated foreign propositions into undigested Hegelian language, or literary gleaners in the "cultural-historical" field, like Herr Riehl. The final outcome of this was cameralism,[1] a mush consisting of all sorts of extraneous matter, with a spattering of eclectic-economic sauce, such as would be useful knowledge for a young law school graduate in the employ of the state preparing for his final state board examination.

While then the bourgeoisie, schoolmasters and bureaucracy were still laboring to learn the first elements of English-French economics by heart as unassailable dogmas and to attain some degree of clarity about them, the German proletarian party appeared on the scene. Its whole theoretical existence proceeded from the study of political economy; and scientific, independent *German economics* dates from the moment of its appearance. This German economics is based essentially upon the materialist conception of history, the basic features of which are presented briefly in the preface to the above-named work. The main points of this preface have already been printed in *Volk*, for which reason we referred to it. Not only for economics, but for all historical sciences (and all sciences which are not natural sciences are historical) a revolutionizing discovery is made with this proposition: "that the mode of production of material life determines the social, political and intellectual life processes in general"; that all the social and political relations, all religious and legal systems, all the theoretical outlooks which emerge in the course of history, are to be comprehended only when the material conditions of life of the respectively corresponding epochs are understood and the former are derived from these material conditions. "It is not the consciousness of men that determines their being; but their social being that determines their consciousness." The proposition is so simple that it must be self-evident to anyone who is not bemused by idealist delusions. But it involves

[1] The word is derived from the chambers that administered state property in Germany.—*Ed.*

highly revolutionary consequences, not only for theory but also for practice.

"At a certain stage of their development the material forces of production in society come into conflict with the existing relations of production or—what is but a legal expression for the same thing—with the property relations within which they have been at work before. From forms of development of the forces of production these relations turn into their fetters. Then begins an epoch of *social revolution*. With the change of the economic foundation the entire immense superstructure is more or less rapidly transformed. . . .

"The bourgeois relations of production are the last antagonistic form of the social process of production—antagonistic not in the sense of individual antagonism, but of one arising from the social conditions of life of the individuals; at the same time the productive forces developing in the womb of bourgeois society create the material conditions for the solution of this antagonism." [1]

As we pursue our materialist thesis further and apply it to the present, the perspective of a tremendous revolution, indeed the most tremendous revolution of all time, therefore immediately unfolds itself before us.

On closer consideration, it is, however, also immediately evident that this apparently simple proposition, that the consciousness of men depends on their being and not *vice versa*, at once, and as its first consequences, runs directly counter to all idealism, even the most concealed. All traditional and customary outlooks on everything historical are negated by it. The whole traditional mode of political reasoning falls to the ground; patriotic noble-mindedness fights indignantly against such an unprincipled conception. The new mode of outlook, therefore, necessarily came into conflict, not only with the representatives of the bourgeoisie, but also with the mass of French socialists who would fain shake the world by means of the magic formula,

[1] Karl Marx, *Contribution to the Critique of Political Economy*, pp. 12-13, Charles H. Kerr & Co., Chicago.

liberté, égalité, fraternité! But above all it aroused great wrath among the German vulgar-democratic screamers. All the same they have by preference attempted to exploit the new ideas in plagiaristic fashion, but with rare misunderstanding.

The development of the materialist conception even in regard to a single historical example was a scientific work which would have demanded years of tranquil study, for it is obvious that nothing can be done here with mere phrases, that only a mass of critically sifted, completely mastered historical material can enable one to solve such a task. The February Revolution thrust our party on the political stage and thereby made it impossible for it to pursue purely scientific aims. Nevertheless, this basic outlook runs like a red thread through all the literary productions of the party. In all of them in each particular case it is demonstrated how every time the action originated from direct material impulses, not from the phrases that accompanied the action, and how, on the contrary, the political and juristic phrases were derived from the material impulses just as much as the political actions and their results.

When, after the defeat of the Revolution of 1848-49, a period began in which it became more and more impossible to influence Germany from without, our party surrendered the field of emigrational quarrels —for that remained the only possible activity—to vulgar democracy. While the latter indulged in intrigues to its heart's content, and squabbled today in order to make up the day after, and the day after that again washed all its dirty linen in view of everyone—while vulgar democracy went begging through the whole of America in order immediately afterwards to stage new scandals over the division of the few pence secured—our party was glad once again to have some leisure for study. It had the great advantage of having a new scientific outlook as its theoretical basis, the working out of which kept it fully occupied; for this reason alone it could never degenerate to such an extent as the "great men" among the emigrants.

The first fruit of these studies is the book under review.

II

In a publication like the one before us there can be no question of a merely desultory criticism of separate chapters taken from political economy, of the isolated treatment of this or that disputed economic question. Rather it is from the outset constructed so as to be a systematic summing up of the whole complex of economic science, interconnected development of the laws of bourgeois production and bourgeois exchange. Since the economists are nothing but the interpreters of and apologists for these laws, this development is at the same time a criticism of the whole of economic literature.

Since Hegel's death hardly any attempt has been made to develop a science in its own inner interconnection. The official Hegelian school had appropriated from the dialectic of the master only the manipulation of the simplest tricks, which it applied to anything and everything, often with ludicrous clumsiness. For it the whole inheritance of Hegel was limited to a mere pattern by the help of which every theme could be correctly devised, and to a compilation of words and turns of speech which had no other purpose than to be inserted at the right time when thought and positive knowledge failed them. Thus it came about that, as a Bonn professor said, these Hegelians understood nothing about anything, but could write about everything. This was certainly the case. Meanwhile, these gentlemen were, in spite of their self-complacency, so conscious of their weakness that they avoided big problems as much as possible. The old pedantic science held the field by its superiority in positive knowledge. And when Feuerbach also gave notice that he was quitting the field of speculative conceptions, Hegelianism quietly fell asleep; and it seemed as if the old metaphysics, with its fixed categories, had begun to reign anew in science.

The thing had its natural cause. After the regime of the Hegelian Diadochi,[1] which had wound up with pure phrases, there naturally

[1] The successors of Hegel—philosophers and Hegelians—who were unable to overcome Hegelian idealism. See pp. 9-19 of this edition.—*Ed.*

followed an epoch in which the positive content of science outweighed its formal side. Germany, too, immersed itself in natural science with a quite extraordinary energy which corresponded with the powerful bourgeois development after 1848. And while these sciences in which the speculative tendency never assumed any kind of importance were in fashion, there was a recrudescence of the old metaphysical manner of thinking up to and including the most extreme insipidities of Wolff.[1]

Hegel fell into oblivion; and there developed the new natural-scientific materialism which was almost indistinguishable theoretically from that of the eighteenth century, and for the most part only enjoyed the advantage of having a richer, natural-scientific material at its disposal, particularly in chemistry and physiology. The narrow, philistine mode of thought of pre-Kantian times one finds reproduced even to the most extreme triviality in Büchner and Vogt; and even Moleschott, who swears by Feuerbach, continually runs amuck in the most diverting fashion among the simplest of categories. The lumbering cart-horse of everyday bourgeois understanding naturally stopped dead in confusion before the ditch which separates essence from appearance, cause from effect. But if one goes gaily hunting over such badly broken ground as that of abstract thinking, one must not ride cart-horses.

Here, therefore, was another problem to be solved, one which had nothing to do with political economy as such. How was science to be treated? On the one hand there was the Hegelian dialectics in the wholly abstract, "speculative" form in which Hegel had bequeathed it; on the other hand there was the ordinary, essentially metaphysical Wolffian method which had again become fashionable and in which the bourgeois economists had written their fat, disjointed tomes. This latter method had been so annihilated theoretically by Kant and particularly by Hegel that only lassitude and the lack of any *simple*

---

[1] *C. Wolff* (1679-1754). German philosopher of the Enlightenment. As an example of his insipidities, Engels cites in the old introduction to *Dialectics of Nature*, p. 7 (International Publishers, New York) Wolff's statement that "cats were created to eat mice, mice to be eaten by cats, and the whole of nature to testify to the wisdom of the creator."—*Ed.*

alternative method could make possible its continued existence in practice. On the other hand the Hegelian method was absolutely unusable in its *available* form. It was essentially idealistic, and the problem here was that of developing a world contemplation more materialistic than any previously advanced. This method started with pure thinking and here one was to start from stubborn facts. A method which, according to its own admission, "came from nothing, through nothing, to nothing," was in this form completely out of place here.

Nevertheless, of all the available logical material, it was the only thing which could be used, at least as a starting point. It had never been criticized, never overcome. Not one of the opponents of the great dialectician had been able to make a breach in its proud structure; it fell into oblivion, because the Hegelian school had not the slightest notion of what to do with it. It was, therefore, above all necessary to subject the Hegelian method to thorough-going criticism.

What distinguished Hegel's mode of thought from that of all other philosophers was the enormous historical sense upon which it was based. Abstract and idealist though it was in form, yet the development of his thoughts always proceeded in line with the development of world history and the latter was really meant to be only the test of the former. If, thereby, the real relation was inverted and stood on its head, nevertheless, the real content entered everywhere into the philosophy: all the more so since Hegel—in contrast to his disciples— did not parade ignorance, but was one of the finest intellects of all time. He was the first who attempted to show an evolution, an inner coherence, in history; and while today much in his *Philosophy of History* may seem peculiar to us, yet the grandeur of his fundamental outlook is admirable even today, whether one makes comparison with his predecessors, or with anyone who, since his time, has taken the liberty of reflecting in general concerning history. Everywhere, in his *Phenomenology, Aesthetics, History of Philosophy,* this magnificent conception of history penetrates, and everywhere this material is treated historically, in a definite, even if abstractly distorted, inter-connection with history.

This epoch-making conception of history was the direct theoretical prerequisite for the new materialist contemplation, and thereby already provided a connecting point for the logical method. Since this forgotten dialectics had led to such results even from the standpoint of "pure thinking," and had, in addition, so easily settled accounts with all preceding logic and metaphysics, there must of necessity have been something more to it than sophistry and hair-splitting. But the criticism of this method, which all officially recognized philosophy had fought shy of and still does, was no trifle.

Marx was, and is, the only one who could undertake the work of extracting from the Hegelian logic the kernel which comprised Hegel's real discoveries in this sphere, and to construct the dialectical method, divested of its idealistic trappings, in the simple shape in which it becomes the only true form of development of thought. The working out of the method which forms the foundation of Marx's *Contribution to the Critique of Political Economy* we consider a result of hardly less importance than the basic materialist outlook itself.[1]

The criticism of economics, even according to the method secured, could still be exercised in two ways: historically or logically. Since in history, as in its literary reflection, development as a whole proceeds from the most simple to the more complex relations, the historical development of the literature of political economy provided a natural guiding thread with which criticism could link up and the economic categories as a whole would thereby appear in the same sequence as in the logical development. This form apparently has the advantage of greater clearness, since indeed it is the *actual* development that is followed, but as a matter of fact it would thereby at most become more popular. History often proceeds by jumps and zigzags and it would in this way have to be followed everywhere, whereby not only would

---

[1] The working out of the method was also achieved by Lenin. His so-called "philosophical notebooks" provide most valuable material for the materialist use of Hegelian dialectics—*Ed*.

much material of minor importance have to be incorporated, but there would be much interruption of the chain of thought; furthermore, the history of economics could not be written without that of bourgeois society and this would make the task endless, since all preliminary work is lacking. The logical method of treatment was, therefore, the only appropriate one. But this, as a matter of fact, is nothing else than the historical method; only divested of its historical form and disturbing fortuities. The chain of thought must begin with the same thing with which this history begins and its further course will be nothing else than the mirror-image of the historical course in abstract and theoretically consistent form; a corrected mirror-image but corrected according to laws furnished by the real course of history itself, in that each factor can be considered at its ripest point of development, in its classic form.

In this method we proceed from the first and simplest relation that historically and in fact confronts us; here, therefore, from the first economic relation to be found. We analyze this relation. Being a *relation* already implies that it has two sides, *related to each other*. Each of these sides is considered by itself; which brings us to the way they behave to each other, their reciprocal interaction. Contradictions will result which demand a solution. But as we are not considering an abstract process of thought taking place solely in our heads, but a real happening which has actually taken place at some particular time, or is still taking place, these contradictions, too, will have developed in practice and will probably have found their solution. We shall trace the nature of this solution, and shall discover that it has been brought about by the establishment of a new relation whose two opposite sides we shall now have to develop, and so on.

Political economy begins with *commodities,* begins from the moment when products are exchanged for one another—whether by individuals or by primitive communities. The product that appears in exchange is a commodity. It is, however, a commodity solely because a *relation* between two persons or communities attaches to the *thing,* the product, the relation between producer and consumer who are here no longer united in the same person. Here at once we have an example of a peculiar fact, which runs through the whole of economics and which has caused utter confusion in the minds of the bourgeois economists: economics deals not with things but with relations between persons, and, in the last resort, between classes; these relations are, however, always *attached to things* and *appear as things*. This interconnection, which in isolated cases it is true has dawned upon individual economists, was first discovered by Marx as obtaining for all political economy, whereby he made the most difficult questions so simple and clear that now even the bourgeois economists will be able to grasp them.

If now we consider commodities from their various aspects, commodities in their complete development and not as they first laboriously developed in the primitive barter between two primitive communities, they present themselves to us from the two points of view of use value and exchange value, and here we at once enter the sphere of economic dispute. Anyone who would like to have a striking illustration of the fact that the German dialectical method in its present state of elaboration is at least as superior to the old, shallow, garrulous metaphysical method as the railway is to the means of transport of the Middle Ages should read in Adam Smith or any other reputable official economist what a torment exchange value and use value were to these gentlemen, how difficult it was for them to keep them properly apart and to comprehend each in its peculiar distinctness, and should then compare the simple, clear treatment by Marx.

After use value and exchange value have been developed, commodities are presented as the immediate unity of both, in the form in which they enter *the process of exchange*. What contradictions result here can afterwards be read on pp. 20, 21.[1] We only notice that these contradictions are not merely of abstract theoretical interest, but at the same time reflect the difficulties which emerge from the nature of the immediate exchange relations, of simple barter, reflect the impossi-

[1] Engels refers here to the pages of Marx's book, *A Contribution to the Critique of Political Economy.—Ed.*

bilities in which this first crude form of exchange necessarily terminates. The solution of these impossibilities is to be found in the fact that the property of representing the exchange value of all other commodities is transferred to a special commodity—*money*. Money or simple circulation is now developed in the second chapter, *viz.*, 1) money as the *measure of value*, in which connection the value measured in money, the *price*, receives its closer determination; 2) as *means of circulation* and 3) as the unity of both determinations, as *real money*, as the representative of all material bourgeois wealth. This closes the development of the first booklet, reserving the passing of money into capital for the second.

It is seen that with this method the logical development is by no means compelled to keep to the purely abstract sphere. On the contrary, this method requires historical illustrations, continual contact with reality. Such proofs are accordingly introduced in great variety, namely references both to the actual course of history at different stages of social development and also to the economic literature in which the clear working out of the determinations of economic relations is pursued from the beginning. The criticism of individual more or less one-sided or confused modes of conception is then in essence already given in the logical development itself and can be briefly formulated.

In a third article we shall deal with the economic content of the book itself. (*See* note on page 70 of this volume.—*Ed.*)

Karl Marx

Theses on Feuerbach [1]

I

THE chief defect of all hitherto existing materialism—that of Feuerbach included—is that the object, reality, sensuousness, is conceived only in the form of the *object* or *contemplation* [2] but not as *human sensuous activity, practice,* not subjectively. Thus it happened that the *active* side, in opposition to materialism, was developed by idealism— but only abstractly, since, of course, idealism does not know real sensuous activity as such. Feuerbach wants sensuous objects, really differentiated from the thought-objects, but he does not conceive human activity itself as activity *through objects.* Consequently, in the *Essence of Christianity,* he regards the theoretical attitude as the only genuinely human attitude, while practice is conceived and fixed only in its dirty-Jewish form of appearance. Hence he does not grasp the significance of "revolutionary," of practical-critical, activity.

II

The question whether objective truth can be attributed to human thinking is not a question of theory but is a practical question. In practice man must prove the truth, *i.e.,* the reality and power, the "this-sidedness" of his thinking. The dispute over the reality or non-reality of thinking which is isolated from practice is a purely scholastic question.

[1] The "Theses on Feuerbach" written by Marx in Brussels in the spring of .845 were found by Engels in an old notebook left by Marx, forty years after they were written. As they were not in a finished form, Engels prepared them for publication.—*Ed.*

[2] German—*Anschauung.*—*Ed.*

III

The materialist doctrine that men are products of circumstances and upbringing and that, therefore, changed men are products of other circumstances and changed upbringing forgets that circumstances are changed precisely by men and that the educator must himself be educated. Hence this doctrine necessarily arrives at dividing society into two parts, of which one towers above society (in Robert Owen, for example).

The coincidence of the changing of circumstances and of human activity can only be conceived and rationally understood as revolutionizing practice.

IV

Feuerbach starts out from the fact of religious self-alienation, the duplication of the world into a religious, imaginary world and a real one. His work consists in the dissolution of the religious world into its secular basis. He overlooks the fact that after completing this work, the chief thing still remains to be done. For the fact that the secular foundation lifts itself above itself and establishes itself in the clouds as an independent realm is only to be explained by the self-cleavage and self-contradictoriness of this secular basis. The latter must itself, therefore, first be understood in its contradiction and then, by the removal of the contradiction, revolutionized in practice. Thus, for instance, once the earthly family is discovered to be the secret of the holy family, the former must then itself be theoretically criticized and radically changed in practice.

V

Feuerbach, not satisfied with *abstract thinking*, appeals to *sensuous contemplation*, but he does not conceive sensuousness as a practical, human-sensuous activity.

VI

Feuerbach resolves the religious essence into the human. But the human essence is no abstraction inherent in each single individual. In its reality it is the *ensemble* of the social relations.

Feuerbach, who does not attempt the criticism of this real essence, is consequently compelled:

1. To abstract from the historical process and to fix the religious sentiment as something for itself and to presuppose an abstract—*isolated*—human individual.

2. The human essence, therefore, can with him be comprehended only as "genus," as a dumb internal generality which merely *naturally* unites the many individuals.

VII

Feuerbach, consequently, does not see that the "religious sentiment" is itself a *social product,* and that the abstract individual whom he analyzes belongs in reality to a particular form of society.

VIII

Social life is essentially *practical.* All mysteries which mislead theory to mysticism find their rational solution in human practice and in the comprehension of this practice.

IX

The highest point attained by contemplative materialism, *i.e.,* materialism which does not understand sensuousness as practical activity, is the outlook of single individuals in "civil society." [1]

X

The standpoint of the old materialism is "civil society"; the standpoint of the new is *human* society or socialized humanity.

XI

The philosophers have *interpreted* the world in various ways; the point however is to *change* it.

---

[1] Here not "bourgeois society," but "civil society" [bürgerliche Gesellschaft], as in Hegel, in the sense of the totality of social (economic, personal, cultural, etc.) relations, as distinguished from the political organism, the state.—*Ed.*

Karl Marx

On the History of French Materialism [1]

"TO speak in an exact and prosaic sense," the French enlightenment of the eighteenth century, particularly French materialism, was not only a struggle against the existing political institutions as well as against the existing religion and theology but was quite as much an open, outspoken struggle against the metaphysics of the seventeenth century and against all metaphysics, especially that of Descartes, Malebranche, Spinoza and Leibniz. Philosophy was set up in opposition to metaphysics; just as Feuerbach, when he first came out decidedly against Hegel, placed sober philosophy in opposition to intoxicated speculation. The metaphysics of the seventeenth century, which were swept from the field by the French enlightenment and particularly by French materialism of the eighteenth century, lived to see its triumphant and substantial restoration in German philosophy, and especially in the speculative German philosophy of the nineteenth century. After Hegel, in brilliant style, had combined it with all subsequent metaphysics and with German idealism and had founded a universal kingdom of metaphysics, the attack on speculative metaphysics and on all metaphysics became once again, as in the eighteenth century, equivalent to the attack on theology. Metaphysics will succumb, for good and all, to materialism now completed by the work of speculation itself and coinciding with humanism. French and English socialism and communism represented this coincidence of humanism and materialism in the realm of practice, just as Feuerbach represented it in the theoretical sphere.

"To speak in an exact and prosaic sense," there are two tendencies in

[1] From *The Holy Family.—Ed.*

French materialism, of which one derives its origin from Descartes and the other from Locke. The latter is preeminently an element of French culture and flows directly into socialism. The former, mechanical materialism, merges into French natural science proper. Both tendencies intersect in the course of development. We do not need to deal more closely with the French materialism coming direct from Descartes, any more than with the French school of Newton and the development of French natural science in general.

Therefore, only this must need be said: In his physics Descartes had invested matter with self-creative power and had conceived of mechanical motion as its vital act. He had completely separated his physics from his metaphysics. Within his physics matter is the sole substance, the sole basis of being and knowing.

French mechanical materialism attached itself to the physics of Descartes in contrast to his metaphysics. His disciples were by profession anti-metaphysicians, *viz.,* physicians.[1]

This school begins with the physician Leroy; it reaches its acme with the physician Cabanis. The physician Lamettrie is its center. Descartes was still living when Leroy transferred the Cartesian conception of animals to the human soul—as, similarly, Lamettrie did in the eighteenth century—and declared the soul to be a mode of the body and ideas to be mechanical motions. Leroy even believed Descartes had concealed his real opinions. Descartes protested. At the end of the eighteenth century, Cabanis completed Cartesian materialism in his work: *Rapport du physique et du moral de l'homme* [*Report on the Physique and Morality of Man*].

Cartesian materialism exists in France up to the present day. It won its great successes in mechanical natural science, which, to speak in an exact and prosaic sense, will least of all be reproached with being romantic.

The metaphysics of the seventeenth century, as represented in France particularly by Descartes, had materialism as an antagonist from the hour of its birth. This antagonism to Descartes was personified in

[1] In the sense of physicist.—*Ed.*

Gassendi, the restorer of Epicurean materialism. French and English materialism always remained in close relationship to Democritus and Epicurus. Cartesian metaphysics had another opponent in the English materialist Hobbes. Gassendi and Hobbes vanquished their opponent long after their death at the very moment when Cartesian metaphysics already ruled as the official power in all French schools.

Voltaire has remarked that the indifference of the French in the eighteenth century to the quarrels between Jesuits and Jansenists resulted less from philosophy than from Law's financial speculations. Thus the overthrow of the metaphysics of the seventeenth century can be attributed to the materialist theory of the eighteenth century only in so far as this theoretical movement is itself explained by the practical form of French life at that time. This life was directed to the immediate present, to worldly enjoyment and worldly interests, to the earthly world. Anti-theological, anti-metaphysical, materialist theories necessarily corresponded to its anti-theological, its anti-metaphysical, its materialist practice. Metaphysics has lost practically all credit. Here we need only briefly indicate its theoretical course.

In the seventeenth century metaphysics was still saturated with positive, profane content (see Descartes, Leibniz, etc.). It made discoveries in mathematics, physics and other exact sciences which appeared to belong to it. By the beginning of the eighteenth century this semblance had already been destroyed. The positive sciences had separated themselves from it and had marked off their independent domain. The whole wealth of metaphysics now consisted in nothing but thought-entities and heavenly things, at precisely the time when real entities and earthly things began to concentrate all attention upon themselves. Metaphysics had become stale. Helvetius and Condillac were born in the same year that Malebranche and Arnauld, the last great French metaphysicians of the seventeenth century, died.

The man who ruined the theoretical credit of the metaphysics of the seventeenth century and of all metaphysics was Pierre Bayle. His weapon was skepticism, forged out of the magical formulae of metaphysics itself. He himself took Cartesian metaphysics as his immediate starting point. Just as Feuerbach, by combating speculative theology, was driven further to combating speculative philosophy, precisely because he recognized speculation to be the last support of theology, because he had to drive the theologians back from pseudo-science to crude, repellent faith, so religious doubt forced Bayle into doubting the metaphysics which supported this faith. Metaphysics, therefore, in its entire historical· evolution, was subjected by him to criticism. Bayle became its historian in order to write the history of its death. Above all he refuted Spinoza and Leibniz.

Pierre Bayle not only prepared the way for the acceptance in France of materialism and common-sense philosophy by the skeptical disintegration of metaphysics. He heralded the atheistic society which was soon to come into existence, by proving that a society of sheer atheists was existing; that an atheist could be an honorable man; that man degraded himself not by atheism but by superstition and idolatry.

In the words of a French writer, Pierre Bayle was "the last metaphysician in the sense of the seventeenth century and the first philosopher in the sense of the eighteenth century."

In addition to the negative refutation of the theology and metaphysics of the seventeenth century, a positive anti-metaphysical system was needed. A book was required which would systematize the practical activities of the time and give them a theoretical foundation. Locke's *Essay Concerning the Origin of the Human Understanding* came from the other side of the channel as if at call. It was greeted enthusiastically like an eagerly awaited guest.

The question arises: Is Locke perhaps a disciple of Spinoza? "Profane" history might answer:[1]

"Materialism is the natural-born son of Great Britain. Already the British schoolman, Duns Scotus, asked, 'whether it was impossible for matter to think.'

"In order to effect this miracle, he took refuge in god's omnipotence,

[1] The following paragraphs are taken from Frederick Engels' quotation of them in English in the Introduction to his *Socialism: Utopian and Scientific*, pp. 10-12, International Publishers, New York.—*Ed.*

i.e., he made theology preach materialism. Moreover, he was a nominalist. Nominalism, the first form of materialism, is chiefly found among the English schoolmen.

"The real progenitor of English materialism is Bacon. To him natural philosophy is the only true philosophy, and physics based upon the experience of the senses in the chiefest part of natural philosophy. Anaxagoras and his homoeomeria, Democritus and his atoms, he often quotes as his authorities. According to him the senses are infallible and the source of all knowledge. All science is based on experience, and consists in subjecting the data furnished by the senses to a rational method of investigation. Induction, analysis, comparison, observation, experiment are the principal forms of such a rational method. Among the qualities inherent in matter, motion is the first and foremost, not only in the form of mechanical and mathematical motion, but chiefly in the form of an impulse, a vital spirit, a tension—or a *"qual,"* to use a term of Jacob Böhme's [1]—of matter.

"In Bacon, its first creator, materialism still occludes within itself the germs of a many-sided development. On the one hand, matter, surrounded by a sensuous, poetic glamour, seems to attract man's whole entity by winning smiles. On the other, the aphoristically formulated doctrine pullulates with inconsistencies imported from theology.

"In its further evolution materialism becomes one-sided. Hobbes is the man who systematizes Baconian materialism. Knowledge based upon the senses loses its poetic blossom, it passes into the abstract experience of the mathematician; geometry is proclaimed as the queen of sciences. Materialism takes to misanthropy. If it is to overcome its opponent, misanthropic, fleshless spiritualism, and that on the latter's own ground, materialism has to chastise its own flesh and turn ascetic. Thus, from a sensual it passes into an intellectual entity; but thus, too, it evolves all the consistency, regardless of consequences, characteristic of the intellect.

[1] "*'Qual'* is a philosophical play upon words. *Qual* literally means torture, a pain which drives to action of some kind; at the same time the mystic Böhme puts into the German word something of the meaning of the Latin *qualitas;* his *'qual'* was the activating principle arising from, and promoting in its turn, the spontaneous development of the thing, relation, or person subject to it, in contradistinction to a pain inflicted from without."

"Hobbes, as Bacon's continuator, argues thus: if all human knowledge is furnished by the senses, then our concepts and ideas are but the phantoms, divested of their sensual forms, of the real world. Philosophy can but give names to these phantoms. One name may be applied to more than one of them. There may even be names of names. It would imply a contradiction if, on the one hand, we maintained that all ideas had their origin in the world of sensation, and, on the other, that a word was more than a word; that besides the beings known to us by our senses, beings which are one and all individuals, there existed also beings of a general, not individual, nature. An unbodily substance is the same absurdity as an unbodily body. Body, being, substance, are but different terms for the same reality. *It is impossible to separate thought from matter that thinks.* This matter is the substratum of all changes going on in the world. The word 'infinite' is meaningless, unless it states that our mind is capable of performing an endless process of addition. Only material things being perceptible to us, we cannot know anything about the existence of god. My own existence alone is certain. Every human passion is a mechanical movement which has a beginning and an end. The objects of impulse are what we call good. Man is subject to the same laws as nature. Power and freedom are identical.

"Hobbes had systematized Bacon, however, furnishing a proof for Bacon's fundamental principle, the origin of all human knowledge from the world of sensation. It was Locke who, in his *Essay Concerning the Origin of the Human Understanding,* supplied this proof.

"Hobbes had shattered the theistic prejudices of Baconian materialism; Collins, Dodwell, Coward, Hartley and Priestley similarly shattered the last theological bars that still hemmed in Locke's sensationalism. At all events, for practical materialists, theism is but an easy-going way of getting rid of religion."

We have mentioned already at how opportune a time Locke's work came to the French. Locke had given a basis to the philosophy of *bon sens,* of common sense; that is to say: put in a roundabout way, that there is no philosophy other than that of the normal human senses and the understanding based on them.

Condillac, who was Locke's immediate pupil and his interpreter in French, at once turned Locke's sensationalism against seventeenth century metaphysics. He proved that the French were correct in rejecting metaphysics as being a mere figment of the imagination and of theological prejudices. He published a refutation of the systems of Descartes, Spinoza, Leibniz and Malebranche. In his work *L'essai sur l'origine des connaissances humaines* (*Essay Concerning the Origin of Human Knowledge.—Ed.*), he gave an exposition of Locke's ideas and proved that not only the soul but also the senses, not only the art of creating ideas but also the art of sensuous perception are matters of experience and habit. The entire development of man, therefore, depends upon upbringing and external circumstances. Condillac was supplanted in the French schools only by eclectic philosophy.

The difference between French and English materialism is the difference between the two nationalities. The French endowed English materialism with *esprit,* with flesh and blood, with eloquence. They gave it the temperament and grace which was still lacking. They civilized it.

In Helvetius, who likewise started out from Locke, materialism receives its real French character. He comprehended it at once in its relation to social life. (Helvetius, *De l'homme* [*On Man*].) Sensuous qualities and egoism, pleasure and enlightened self-interest are the foundation of all morality. The natural equality of human intelligences, the unity between the progress of reason and the progress of industry, the natural goodness of man, the omnipotence of upbringing are the principal features of his system.

A combination of Cartesian and English materialism is to be found in the writings of Lamettrie. He uses the physics of Descartes to its minutest detail. His *L'homme-machine* [*Man-Machine.—Ed.*] is a performance on the model of the *Tier-Maschine* [*Animal-Machine*] of Descartes. In Holbach's *Systéme de la nature* [*System of Nature*] the section on physics likewise consists of a combination of French and English materialism, just as the section on morals rests essentially on the morality of Helvetius. Robinet (*De la nature*), the French materialist who most of all still remained connected with metaphysics, and was also praised for this by Hegel, expressly made reference to Leibniz.

Now that we have established the double derivation of French materialism from Cartesian physics and English materialism, and also the antithesis between French materialism and the metaphysics of the seventeenth century—the metaphysics of Descartes, Spinoza, Malebranche and Leibniz—we do not need to speak of Volney, Dupuis, Diderot, any more than of the physiocrats. This antithesis could become apparent to the Germans only after they themselves had come into conflict with speculative metaphysics.

Just as Cartesian materialism issues into natural science proper, so the other tendency in French materialism flows directly into socialism and communism.

No great acumen is required to perceive the necessary interconnection of materialism with communism and socialism, from the doctrines of materialism concerning the original goodness and equal intellectual endowment of man; concerning the omnipotence of experience, habit and upbringing; concerning the influence of external circumstances on man, the great importance of industry, the justification of enjoyment, etc. If man constructs all his knowledge, perception, etc., from the world of sense and his experiences in the world of sense, then it follows that it is a question of so arranging the empirical world that he experiences the truly human in it, that he becomes accustomed to experiencing himself as a human being.

If enlightened self-interest is the principle of all morality, it follows that the private interests of men ought to be made to coincide with human interests. If man is unfree in the material sense—that is, is free not by reason of the negative force of being able to avoid this or that, but by reason of the positive power to assert his true individuality, then one should not punish individuals for crimes but rather destroy the anti-social breeding places of crime, and give every person social room for the necessary assertion of his or her vitality. If man is formed by circumstances, then the circumstances must be formed humanly. If man is social by nature then he develops his true nature only in society; hence the power of his nature must be measured not by the power of a single individual but by the power of society.

One finds these and similar propositions almost word for word even in the oldest of the French materialists. This is not the place to express an opinion on them. Significant of the socialist tendency of materialism is the apology for vice by Mandeville, one of the oldest English disciples of Locke. He proves that vice is indispensable and useful in present-day society, which is no apology for present-day society.

Fourier proceeds directly from the doctrines of French materialism. The followers of Babeuf were crude, uncivilized materialists, but even developed communism derives directly from French materialism. French materialism in the form which Helvetius had given it returns to its native home, England. Upon the morality of Helvetius, Bentham founds his system of enlightened self-interest, just as Owen, proceeding from Bentham, gave a basis to English communism. On being banished to England, the Frenchman Cabet is stimulated by communist ideas found there and returns to France to become the most popular, if also the most shallow, representative of communism. The more scientific French Communists—Dezamy, Gay, etc.—like Owen, develop the teachings of materialism as the doctrine of real humanism and as the logical basis of communism.

Note: The connection between French materialism, and Descartes and Locke, and the antithesis between the philosophy of the eighteenth century and the metaphysics of the seventeenth century are dealt with in detail in most recent French histories of philosophy. Here, as against critical criticism, we had only to repeat that which was known. On the other hand, the interconnection between the materialism of the eighteenth century and the English and French communism of the nineteenth century still needs a detailed presentation. Here we confine ourselves to the quotation of a few, short, pregnant excerpts from Helvetius, Holbach and Bentham.

1. *Helvetius.* "Men are not bad, but are made subject to their interests. One must not, therefore, complain about the wickedness of men, but about the ignorance of the law-makers, who have continually placed the particular interest in antagonism to the general interest."

"The moralists have hitherto had no success because one has to dig deep into legislation in order to tear out the creative roots of vice. In New Orleans women may repudiate their husbands as soon as they are tired of them. In such lands there are no false wives, because they have no interest in being such."

"Morality is only a frivolous science if it is not combined with politics and legislation. One recognizes the hypocritical moralists on the one hand in the indifference with which they regard the vices that disintegrate empires, and on the other hand in the passionate anger with which they rage against private vices."

"Men are born neither good nor bad, but ready to be one or the other, according as they are united or divided by a common interest. If the citizens were unable to realize their particular well-being without realizing the general well-being, there would be no wicked people except fools." (*De l'Esprit* [*On the Spirit*], Paris, 1822, I, pp. 117, 240, 291, 299, 351, 369 and 399.)

Just as, according to Helvetius, upbringing, by which (*cf.* I, p. 390) he means not upbringing in the ordinary sense, but the totality of the conditions of the life of an individual, forms man; if a reform is necessary which removes the contradiction between particular interests and general interests, then it requires on the other hand a transformation of the consciousness for the carrying through of such a reform: "great reforms can only be effected by weakening the peoples' stupid veneration for old laws and customs" (p. 260, I.c.), or as he puts it elsewhere, by removing ignorance.

2. *Holbach:* "It is only himself that a man can love in the objects which he loves; it is only himself that he can cherish in the beings of his species.... Man can never, at any moment of his life, separate himself from himself; he can never lose sight of himself.... It is only our advantage, our interests... which causes us to love objects or to hate

them." (*Système Social*, Part I, Paris, 1822, p. 80, 112.) But "man must in his own interests love other men because they are necessary to his own well-being, ... Morality proves to him that of all beings man is the most necessary to man." (P. 76.)

"True morality, like true politics, is that which seeks to bring men nearer to each other with the aim of causing them, by united endeavors, to work for their mutual happiness. Every morality, which separates our interests from those of our fellows, is a false, senseless morality, contrary to nature." (P. 116.)

"To love others ... means to unite our interests with those of our fellows in order to work for the general good. ... Virtue is only the advantage of men united in society." (P. 77.)

"A man without passion or desires would cease to be a man. ... Could one cause a being that is completely detached from itself to be devoted to another being? A man who is indifferent about everything, who is deprived of passions, who is sufficient unto himself, would no longer be a sociable being. ... Virtue is merely the sharing of happiness." (P. 118.)

"Religious morality never served to make mortals more sociable." (P. 36.)

3. *Bentham.* From Bentham we give only one quotation in which he combats the "general interest in the political sense." "The interests of the individual ... should give way to public interests. But ... what does that mean? Is not every individual as much a part of the public as any other? This public interest, which you personify, it is only an abstract expression: it represents only the mass of individual interests. ... If it were good to sacrifice the happiness of an individual in order to increase that of the others, then it would be still better to sacrifice the happiness of a second, of a third, without being able to set any limit. ... Individual interests are the only real interests." (Bentham, *Theory of Rewards and Punishments,* etc., Paris, 1835, third ed., II, p. 230.)